D1711674

THE GANG'S ALL HERE

The Gang's All Here

A PLAY

by Jerome Lawrence and Robert E. Lee

THE WORLD PUBLISHING COMPANY

CLEVELAND AND NEW YORK

Published by The World Publishing Company

2231 West 110th Street, Cleveland 2, Ohio

Published simultaneously in Canada by

Nelson, Foster & Scott Ltd.

Foreword

(This article, by the playwrights, appeared in the New York *Herald Tribune* on September 27, 1959, the Sunday before the play's New York opening.)

Once every four years we get a chance to make history. We go into a voting booth, close the canvas curtain behind us, pull a lever or make an X, and the consequences of what we do will be remembered as long as the English language is spoken or written.

That time is almost here again. The Presidential hopefuls are making their shy denials, and the hyperthyroid campaign Barnums are kicking up a preconvention ruckus. The political air has the brittle snap of first-night anticipation. The box office is already open for America's greatest quadrennial show, and the follow spot is preparing to seek the man who will go to 1600 Pennsylvania Avenue.

In *The Gang's All Here* we are trying to catch some of the high excitement and drama which will fill the national scene in the months ahead. On the cusp of a convention year, we are looking at another convention, an imaginary one. We are examining a White House-bound human being, also imaginary. We are taking a long look at the men who surround a President, the cronies who can become more powerful than kings.

Inauguration Day is much simpler than a Coronation at Westminster Abbey. Yet it makes a phenomenal change in the man who says "So help me God." Many of our Presidents, perhaps most of them, have been rocketed into the White House with almost no preparation. Often they arrive with a hopeless misconception of what is expected of them. How does it feel to stand alone in the Chief Executive's office for the first time?

Our play is not about *a* President, or *the* President, but about the Presidency itself: the father image, the godhead we send to Washington. The great American legend is that every boy can grow up to be President. But what happens to the man-boy? What happens, in particular, if he never should have been elected in the first place; if he sweeps in on his good looks, his "Hail! Hail! The Gang's All Here" personality?

We have stripped any partisan label from our central character. Our politicos are either Republicans or Democrats—it does not matter which. The cigar butts in the caucuses of both parties smell pretty much the same. And the stench of expediency is no more fragrant around a donkey than an elephant.

Is "government by crony" inevitable? We burden our Presidents with such responsibility that only a genius can comprehend the job, and only an archangel can perform it. Hence, we are governed by appointees. Who can blame a man in the White House for choosing people he *knows* to be near him? Prime question: what kind of people does he know?

If Griffith P. Hastings of our play happens to resemble, in part, a President during the rememberable past, he also combines traits of many Presidents. For us to deny that the character is drawn from one President in particular, is perhaps as foolish as for anybody else to insist that he *is* one President in particular. In our preface to *Inherit the Wind,* we say: "This does not pretend to be journalism. It is theatre." The same preface applies to *The Gang's All Here.*

We ask the playgoer's permission to set us free from the restraint of *mere* facts. We hope you will see on the stage of the Ambassador people you can identify, not with remote names in books and newspapers, but with the forces we feel at work in twentieth-century democracy.

If the man we fondly X'd in a voting booth turns out to be a struggling incompetent, whose fault is it? The President's? Not if he really tries, and gains each day in self-knowledge. It's too easy to blame the gang around him, because opportunists are always waiting to fill any governmental vacuum. Perhaps the real trouble lies in our own reluctance to think about history except on that November Tuesday. When we push aside the little canvas curtain and leave the voting booth, the show isn't over. That's when the big curtain is going up.

JEROME LAWRENCE
ROBERT E. LEE

THE GANG'S ALL HERE *was first presented on Broadway by Kermit Bloomgarden Productions, Inc., in association with Sylvia Drulie, at the Ambassador Theatre on October 1, 1959, with the following cast:*

(In order of appearance)

WALTER RAFFERTY	E. G. Marshall
JOSHUA LOOMIS	Bernard Lenrow
CHARLES WEBSTER	Paul McGrath
TAD	Bill Zuckert
HIGGY	Howard Smith
JUDGE CORRIGLIONE	Victor Kilian
DOC KIRKABY	Fred Stewart
FRANCES GREELEY HASTINGS	Jean Dixon
GRIFFITH P. HASTINGS	Melvyn Douglas
COBB	Edwin Cooper
MAID	Anne Shropshire
BRUCE BELLINGHAM	Arthur Hill
ARTHUR ANDERSON	Bram Nossen
AXEL MALEY	Bert Wheeler
LAVERNE	Yvette Vickers
RENEE	Alberta MacDonald
PIANO PLAYER	John Harkins
JOHN BOYD	Clay Hall

Directed by George Roy Hill

Settings and lighting by Jo Mielziner

Costumes by Patricia Zipprodt

Production Stage Manager: Kermit Kegley

Stage Manager: Clifford Cothren

Production Aide: William Barnes

The Time: Quite a while ago.

Act One

Scene 1: A hotel room in Chicago. Past midnight during a political convention.

Scene 2: The Executive Suite, 1600 Pennsylvania Avenue, Washington.

Act Two

Scene 1: A basement room on L Street in Washington.
Scene 2: The Executive Suite.

Act Three

The Presidential Suite of a hotel in San Francisco.

THE GANG'S ALL HERE

ACT ONE

In the dark, we hear the restless noise from the floor of a political convention. A gavel sounds, and the weary voice of the CHAIRMAN *pleads for attention.*

CHAIRMAN'S VOICE Before adjourning for the night, the chair appeals to every delegate to this great convention to break the deadlock between the distinguished General Simpkins and the Honorable Governor of Massachusetts. If we don't, we may all be here till Election Day. On the seventeenth ballot tomorrow morning, *please* let's nominate the next President of the United States so we can all go home! (*Gavel again*) Convention stands adjourned until nine-thirty A.M.

Scene: The sound fades away, and the lights come up on a hotel room in Chicago. It is long past midnight, and the air is sleepy with cigar smoke. The background is an impression of the entire hotel, with squares of light from other windows which blink out one by one during the scene. There is a clutter of coffee cups and sandwich crusts, cigar butts are in the ash trays, and on a side table is a naked bottle of Prohibition whisky, almost empty. A chromo of "The Gleaners" hangs above the rumpled bed. The ceiling presses down on the room, intensifying the heat and the tobacco smell. WALTER RAFFERTY *is alone, playing solitaire on the back of a suitcase. This is a lean, Cassius-looking man—a professional politico of the Enlightened Twenties. He turns up the cards idly, but he is biting hard on*

15

the stem of a rakish cigarette holder. JOSHUA LOOMIS *hurries in, clicking the door shut behind him. An amiable Senator with the drawl of the big ranch country, he seems baited and tired.*

LOOMIS   The whole hotel is going crazy. What the hell are you doing, Walt?

RAFFERTY   Waiting.

LOOMIS   (*Fixing himself a drink*)   Well, I can't wait much longer. The oil boys from San Antonio rented me a seven-room suite on the top floor. There are so many people up there trying to see me, I can't even get in.

RAFFERTY   I've got room for you, Senator. For you—and all your votes.

LOOMIS   (*Takes list from coat pocket*)   Here's a midnight count of how many delegates have switched horses since adjournment.
(RAFFERTY *looks up from the cards, his eyes half-closed*)

RAFFERTY   The Governor is seventy-three votes short of the nomination and the General needs eighty-two.

LOOMIS   Eighty-one. I can't stay uncommitted all night. When are you going to spring our boy?

RAFFERTY   Just relax.
(*The phone rings.* RAFFERTY *leans over and picks up the receiver*)

LOOMIS   If that's San Antonio, I don't want to take it.

RAFFERTY   (*Into the phone*)   Yes? Hello, Charlie.

LOOMIS   Don't tell Charlie Webster I'm here!

RAFFERTY   Yeah. Josh Loomis just dropped in.

LOOMIS You son-of-a-bitch.

RAFFERTY Sure, come on up, Charlie.
(RAFFERTY *hangs up phone*)

LOOMIS I don't want to talk to Webster. I'm having enough
trouble with my people. Some of them think the offers from
his Governor are as sweet as we can get.

RAFFERTY Don't be a damn fool, Josh. You gonna settle for
a handful of post offices when you can have everything?

LOOMIS Do I get Interior? Positively?

RAFFERTY (*Resuming his game of solitaire*) Sometimes you
have to ask for one thing to get another.

LOOMIS What are you going to give yourself?

RAFFERTY Oh, the Justice Department, eventually.

LOOMIS (*Nervously*) Nobody's going to get anything if you
don't start moving.

RAFFERTY When enough palms are sweating, Josh, we'll trot
our dark horse out of the stable.

LOOMIS Does the horse know about it?

RAFFERTY Not yet.

LOOMIS Isn't that a little risky?

RAFFERTY You know him, you've played enough poker with
him. Let me handle it. (*He stops playing with the cards, and
chews on the cigarette holder*) I've been waiting eight years
for tonight. I'm not going to spoil it by rushing. (CHARLES
WEBSTER *appears in the doorway. He is the State Chairman
from Massachusetts, manager of his Governor's campaign.*

WEBSTER *might be mistaken for a banker or a successful corporation executive. But the granite face is worried and the pin-stripe suit is wrinkled with sleeplessness.* RAFFERTY *greets him heartily*) Come on in, Charlie.

WEBSTER (*Entering*) Well, Senator Loomis, has Walt convinced you to swing your votes over to the Governor?

LOOMIS (*Cautiously*) He's been working on me.

WEBSTER Good. Senator, I've gone over your suggestions very carefully. The Governor will do his best to get favorable legislation for your people. And you'll have a post office at practically every cactus bush.
(HIGGY *enters, followed by* TAD. HIGGINS *is a sagging mountain of a man who speaks with the distinctive diction of New Jersey.* TAD, *a jittery delegate in shirt sleeves, has borrowed attention by attaching himself to the mighty* HIGGINS)

TAD We've been waiting upstairs in your suite, Mr. Senator. We didn't know you were down here.

LOOMIS (*Uneasily*) Good evening, gentlemen. Mr. Higgins, I didn't expect to have the campaign managers for the Governor and for the General both paying me a call. Quite an honor.

HIGGY Honor hell. I'm giving you one last chance to climb on the General's bandwagon.

LOOMIS Oh? Has the General decided to make some promises?

HIGGY General Simpkins makes only one promise, to ride up Pennsylvania Avenue and get off at the White House. That's a damn sight more than his Governor'll ever do.
(*Massachusetts and New Jersey glare at each other*)

LOOMIS Do you suppose the General will be riding on horse-back, or in a limousine?

HIGGY What difference does it make?

LOOMIS Well, oats are going out and oil is coming in.

WEBSTER (*Pressing*) Senator Loomis, we've got to have a decision tonight. This deadlock is dangerous. A complete stranger could slip in—some grass roots amateur with nobody behind him but the people. What do you say, Senator?

LOOMIS My instructions are to wait and see what developments occur. (*As* LOOMIS *starts to leave, he meets* DOC *and the* JUDGE *in the doorway*) Good evening, Doctor Kirkaby, Judge Corriglione.

(LOOMIS *escapes.* DOC *is a dry realist with a county-seat sense of humor.* JUDGE CORRIGLIONE *still has a few shreds of the judicial mien, despite a lifetime of losing battles between his conscience and expediency*)

DOC (*Crossing to* WEBSTER) Did you land him, Charlie?

WEBSTER Without Loomis, where do we stand?

DOC Oh. The Governor still needs seventy-three votes.

WEBSTER (*Taking the list from* DOC) All right. Here's what we do. Tomorrow morning, stuff the balcony, get professional cheer leaders. We'll march in and whoop up a demonstration they'll never forgot! We'll drag out those seventy-three votes!

JUDGE So that's how we get a President. Like a touchdown at a football game.

WEBSTER My God, the Governor's almost in!

HIGGY I had a dog once who was almost a thoroughbred.

WEBSTER Your goddamn General is eighty-one votes short of the nomination. Where do you think those votes are coming from?

HIGGY (*Drawing on his cigar*) Eventually, Charles, they're coming from you. When are you gonna unglue those votes you control, and give 'em the man they want? The man our worthy opponents would have run if they'd been smart enough to get him! Simpkins! General Simpkins!

DOC This convention wouldn't nominate General Simpkins if you stuck a saber up his ass and called him Teddy Roosevelt.

HIGGY You come to me with your little poop of a Governor of Massachusetts—

WEBSTER (*Heatedly*) He's a good administrator!
(HIGGY *fetches an envelope out of the pocket of his coat and carelessly tears the canceled stamp off the corner as he speaks*)

HIGGY Here's what I want you to do, Charles. Make me a list of the men in public life who got there just because they were good administrators. Write 'em on the back of this stamp. (*He tosses the torn stamp to* WEBSTER, *then moves to the door like Moby Dick through a swarm of pilot fish*) You smart alecks can sit here all night if you want to. As soon as I pry loose a couple more favorite sons, you gentlemen may be knocking on the door of *my* suite.
(HIGGY *goes out. There is an uncertain pause. Suddenly* TAD *gets up and crosses to the door*)

TAD I'm going along with Higgy.

WEBSTER (*Desperately*) And how many crumbs do you think you'll get from the fat boy's table?

DOC The fact is, the steam's gone out of our boy, Charlie.

TAD What the hell are you gonna do? Pick a name out of a hat?

JUDGE Look gentlemen, there's a point where you have to stop compromising.

WEBSTER Are you going to make a speech, Judge?

JUDGE Yes! A short one. For fifteen minutes can we consider the possibility of nominating the best man?

DOC Your boy got eleven and a half votes on the fourteenth ballot.

TAD God help us. Not another college professor.

JUDGE At least Arthur Anderson is a statesman; not just a vote catcher.

WEBSTER Judge Corriglione. You have not yet arrived in that appointive marble heaven called the Supreme Court, where elections only happen to other people.

JUDGE All I'm asking, Charlie, is how crazy is it to think that the interests of the country and the interests of the party aren't too far apart?

TAD My money's on the General.
(*He crosses toward the door again, but* RAFFERTY *stops him*)

RAFFERTY Tad!
(*When* RAFFERTY *wants attention, he gets it. He is the politician's politician—and when he talks, everybody lis-*

tens. He has a shrewd sense of pause and timing, an earthy eloquence which would be meaningless on a platform but which is brilliant in a smoke-filled room. RAFFERTY *comes downstage and seems to be peering out an imaginary window*)

TAD What are you doing, Rafferty?

RAFFERTY (*Taking a deep breath*) I'm smelling Chicago. (*He leans forward and scans the street eleven stories down*) I'm looking for something, too. And I don't see it. Not one solitary soldier boy. (*He twists a fresh cigarette into the holder*) I do see a young lady who seems to be in an interesting line of work.

(*Drawn by the same curiosity,* WEBSTER, *the* JUDGE, DOC, *and* TAD *join* RAFFERTY *at the window. They look down appreciatively*)

TAD Why doesn't that cop pick her up?

DOC He just did.

RAFFERTY Like hell. She picked *him* up.
(TAD *shrugs and heads for the door again*)

TAD I'm sleepy and I'm hungry. I'm going back to my caucus and recommend the General.

RAFFERTY (*Roaring*) That street down there is *hollering* at you! The General's a soldier and everybody's sick of soldiers, including the soldiers themselves. The cops are sick of being cops. They don't want to run in the "ladies of the evening" —they want to spend the night with them. (*He strides impatiently from one delegate to another*) Four years ago, could we have seen that much of a woman's leg? Fashions change. In politics, too. Four years ago, it was very smart to have

22

the brain showing. But the people who make the X's this November will want a clean-shaven gent with lots of his own hair on top. Everybody's fed up with heroes and angels; they want to come back down here where the good times are. (*A pause. Then he sits on the arm of a chair and speaks with a storyteller's intensity*) I want to tell you something. About eight years ago, I had a startling experience. I was walking down the path in back of the Hotel McKinley in Wilmont, Ohio. I saw a man coming up the path toward me. Forty feet away. But even at that distance, I could see there was something special about him. The power of his walk, the silver majesty of his head. And the eyes—the kind of eyes that seem to be looking directly at you, even if you're 'way at the edge of a crowd. And I said to myself, "Walt Rafferty, you'd better find out who that fella is—because he's got what people vote for. He could be anything—even President of the United States."

JUDGE Well, who was it?

RAFFERTY (*Rising and crossing to the phone*) Operator, let me have Suite 517 please.

WEBSTER (*Worried*) What are you doing, Walt?

RAFFERTY Hello, Frances. Hope I didn't wake you. May I speak to your husband?

WEBSTER (*Fast*) You're acting strictly as an individual, not for any of us.

RAFFERTY Don't wet your pants. Everything's going to be— (*Into phone*) Hello, Griff?

TAD (*Puzzled*) Griff?

RAFFERTY Do I have the honor of addressing Senator Griffith P. Hastings?

 (*They all start talking at once*)

WEBSTER (*Angrily*) If you think you're going to take over this convention—

TAD I can stay awake as long as any of you!

RAFFERTY (*Covering the mouthpiece*) Shut up, everybody! (*There is a sullen silence.* RAFFERTY *speaks blandly into the phone*) Griff, some of the boys are up here in Room 1026— no, Griff, it's not a poker game. (*The* JUDGE *groans*) We just wanted to—well, get your point of view on a few things. We're a long way from a decision, but some of us here have been thinking of you as a possibility. (*He listens, frowns*) Now, Griff. Wait a minute. (*Another pause. He turns his back to the group*) I don't see how you can refuse a thing like this without even talking it over.

WEBSTER Save me from the shy violets.

TAD I saw Hastings make a speech once.

JUDGE *Saw* him make a speech?

TAD He didn't say a damned thing, but he sure looked great.

RAFFERTY (*Hanging up the phone*) He's not interested.

WEBSTER That's a smart act to play, Walt. How long did you rehearse it?

RAFFERTY This late at night Keith's is closed.

DOC (*Pulling on his coat*) I'm going out and get some food.

WEBSTER Call Room Service.

DOC I said food. Not those wooden sandwiches. There's a chop suey joint just off Michigan Boulevard. They give you a cup of wonton soup—with an olive in it. Very dry.

TAD I gotta check with my caucus.

DOC (*Ushering out* TAD *and the* JUDGE) We can do some figuring while we're eating.

TAD Who're you guys gonna try now?

JUDGE Does anybody have a phone number on Rutherford B. Hayes?
(*Webster turns in the doorway*)

WEBSTER Coming, Walt?
(RAFFERTY *leans back thoughtfully in his chair, his hands clasped behind his head*)

RAFFERTY Charlie, you don't like chop suey.
(WEBSTER *closes the door and comes slowly back into the room. These are two king makers of the party; this is a duel by lamplight*)

WEBSTER What does the "P" stand for?

RAFFERTY Huh?

WEBSTER Griffith *P.* Hastings. "President"?

RAFFERTY That's everybody else's middle name.

WEBSTER He's the Senate champ isn't he? Holds the all-time record; hardly ever makes a roll call, never introduced a bill.

RAFFERTY Yep, he's a good party man. Never forgets a face. Never forgets a friend. (*Pause*) Charlie, a long time ago, in the city of Athens, there was a Golden Age. Everybody had everything. And the statesman who ran the show was a fella named Pericles. The schoolbooks say he looked like a god on Olympus. But with no Pericles, there wouldn't have been a Golden Age for anybody.

WEBSTER   Goddamn it, Walt, if we can just find those seventy-three votes.

RAFFERTY   I've got them. I can get them.

WEBSTER   How?

RAFFERTY   Josh Loomis and Griff Hastings are old poker buddies.

WEBSTER   You two-faced bastard! Have you had Loomis in your pocket all along, keeping your mouth shut till you could be king maker? You want to be Higgy?

RAFFERTY   I'm prettier than Higgy. And much easier to do business with.

WEBSTER   What do you want?

RAFFERTY   I just want you to add a four-letter word to your Governor's patriotic aspirations.

WEBSTER   What?

RAFFERTY   Vice. I think he'd make a splendid candidate for *Vice*-President.

WEBSTER   Absolutely not.

RAFFERTY   Charlie, with no effort at all you can lose Ohio.

WEBSTER   Are you working with me or aren't you?

RAFFERTY   I'm just working.

WEBSTER   For Hastings? He turned you down.

RAFFERTY   Charlie, I have elected three Senators and God knows how many Congressmen with one sure-fire technique: They all didn't want it so much they were *sure* to get in.

WEBSTER   Hastings can be Vice-President.

RAFFERTY   Sorry, Charlie.
   (He crosses to the desk.)

WEBSTER   Walt, the Governor's a man of impeccable reputation.

RAFFERTY   Well?

WEBSTER   I've heard some stories about Hastings.

RAFFERTY   Oh?

WEBSTER   Pretty much of a ladies' man, isn't he?

RAFFERTY   They can vote now. The ladies like a ladies' man.

WEBSTER   Yeah. If he's married, with a family, all the trimmings.

RAFFERTY   Griff's married.

WEBSTER   What about the trimmings?

RAFFERTY   Queen Victoria's dead, Charlie.

WEBSTER   Your Senator doesn't make those periodic visits to New York to call on Queen Victoria. She's got a kid, hasn't she?

RAFFERTY   Queen Victoria?

WEBSTER   Damn it, Walt. Is it true?

RAFFERTY   Is what true?

27

WEBSTER   I don't want to find out about any illegitimate child three weeks before Election Day.

RAFFERTY   None of it's true. Take my word for it.

WEBSTER   I believe you. Because you'd be taking one helluva chance if it were true. And if I leave the Governor sitting in the Vice-Presidential outhouse—

RAFFERTY   —what does Charlie Webster get?

WEBSTER   Cabinet?

RAFFERTY   Or equivalent.

WEBSTER   What does that mean? (RAFFERTY *doesn't answer.*) Can I name it?

RAFFERTY   For example?

WEBSTER   The Veterans' Bureau?
  (RAFFERTY *is thoughtful, then nods.*)

RAFFERTY   You can have it.

WEBSTER   Will Hastings approve it?

RAFFERTY   If I say so, your grandmother can be Ambassador to Mexico.

WEBSTER   All right. Now can we pull it off?

RAFFERTY   (*With sudden energy*)   If we stay up all night and work like hell, we can.

WEBSTER   What about Doc and the Judge?

RAFFERTY   Don't worry about them. That's my job. Just hang on to the Governor's votes.
  (*Knock.* RAFFERTY *crosses and opens the door for* FRANCES GREELEY HASTINGS. *She is a handsome woman, a small-town*

patrician for whom Washington is simply an enlarged county seat. Waiting is painful for her, and she has had to wait too much of her life)

FRANCES Mr. Rafferty.

RAFFERTY Why, Mrs. Hastings.
(She comes in, reacting to the intensity of the cigar smoke)

FRANCES I was under the impression that a meeting of delegates was in progress.
(RAFFERTY and WEBSTER exchange glances)

RAFFERTY *(Closing the door)* It's only a recess. With the bad news Griff gave us on the phone, some of the boys had to go out and get braced up.

WEBSTER Sit down, Mrs. Hastings.

RAFFERTY Frances, you know Charles Webster.

FRANCES We met at the banquet of the National Grange, two years ago.

WEBSTER *(Impressed)* Yes.

FRANCES I understand, Walter, that you just made the Senator a very flattering offer.
(There is a pause. RAFFERTY looks at WEBSTER)

RAFFERTY Did we, Charlie?
(Another pause)

WEBSTER I think we can rally the entire party behind your husband, Mrs. Hastings. If he chooses.

FRANCES What about your Governor, Mr. Webster?

WEBSTER He'll take second place on the ticket.

FRANCES Oh?

WEBSTER He's already agreed.

FRANCES And the General?

RAFFERTY He just lost the war.

FRANCES What commitments are involved?

RAFFERTY None.

WEBSTER None whatsoever.

FRANCES (*Taking a deep breath*) Mr. Webster, I have no admiration for women who impose themselves on the political
careers of their husbands. I consider myself only a watcher
But hardly a *disinterested* watcher. (*Turning to* RAFFERTY)
Walter, I believe if you and the leaders of the principal delegations would come to Griffith personally, and appeal to him
on the basis of—

RAFFERTY (*Interrupting*) There's no time, Frances. We'll be
caucusing all night. It'll take three, maybe four ballots tomorrow to clinch this thing.

WEBSTER You want me to go talk to him? What's that room
number?

FRANCES He's not there. He went out for a walk by the lake
front. It would be just as well if the Senator didn't know I
came here. He'd say I was interfering. I'm not. (*With con-
viction*) Whatever decision is made will be entirely his. (*She
turns to* WEBSTER) You see, my husband is a modest man—
(*She breaks off, realizing that* WEBSTER *is no longer looking
at her, but at a figure in the doorway. There's no doubt who
he is: the shock of silver hair, the penetrating eyes, the bear-
ing of an emperor. But* GRIFFITH P. HASTINGS *shatters this*

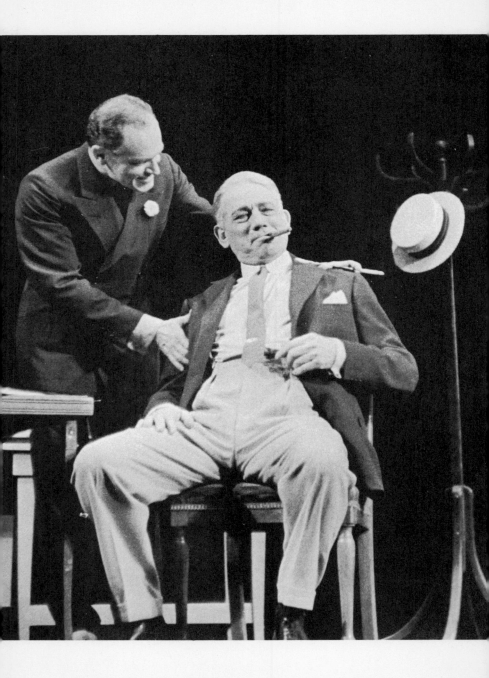

aura of majesty as soon as he opens his mouth in private con-versation)

HASTINGS   I got outside the hotel, took one breath of fresh air, and I realized what the Duchess was up to. (*He passes his wife without speaking, and sits down*) Give me a cigar, will you, Walt? When I breathe smoke, I'd just as soon it was my own.

(RAFFERTY *hands him a cigar.* HASTINGS *bites off the end*)

HASTINGS   Hello, Charlie. Why don't *you* run for President? I'll vote for you.

(WEBSTER *hands* HASTINGS *a small box of matches*)

WEBSTER   Here you are, Senator.

FRANCES   Griffith, if I embarrassed you by coming here—

HASTINGS   Nobody gets embarrassed in politics, Duchess. You get elected or you don't get elected; but you don't get embarrassed. (*Examining the cigar studiously*) Were you serious about that phone call, Walt?

RAFFERTY   Absolutely.

HASTINGS   You want me for a sacrifice play? A bunt to short-stop so the General can get home? I'm willing to do that— if you guarantee I won't get stuck with the nomination.

FRANCES   Griffith doesn't mean that, gentlemen.

HASTINGS   You want to be First Lady, Frances? Go ahead, I'll give you a divorce and you can marry General Simpkins. (*Turning to the others*) The Duchess would make a hell of a First Lady. She's got the stomach for it.

RAFFERTY   Funny thing; I thought every schoolboy in America wanted to be President.

HASTINGS Then get a schoolboy.

RAFFERTY Griff, listen to me. Have I ever steered you wrong?

HASTINGS Couple of times. (*He lights his cigar and grins*) Nothing serious.

RAFFERTY You've trusted me through most of your political career.

HASTINGS (*Simply*) All of it.

RAFFERTY Well, trust me now. I'm not going to feed you a lot of patriotic swill. It's as simple as this: the party wants you, the party needs you.

WEBSTER That's right, Mr. Senator.

HASTINGS (*For the first time, he is completely serious*) For God's sake, Walt, I don't know how to be President!

RAFFERTY Who does? Do you think any backwoods lawyer, or country storekeeper, or half-drunk Civil War General knew any more about it than you do?

HASTINGS Damn it, Walt, don't sell me. I like the Senate. It's the greatest club in the world. "Senator Hastings"! It's got a nice sound to it. But "President Hastings" scares the bejezus out of me. (*Looking around*) You got a bottle around here any place?

RAFFERTY Help yourself.

HASTINGS (*Ignoring it*) In the Senate, up on Capitol Hill, it's like being in a band. You've got ninety-five other fellas tooting the melody along with you. But the President's way out there in front, all by himself—playing solo.

RAFFERTY You won't be alone. You can have your friends with you. The band plays on!

HASTINGS What makes you think I could get elected?

RAFFERTY The man we name tonight, in this room, automatically moves into 1600 Pennsylvania Avenue. (*Pause*) Griff, Griff, when you're sitting on a rocking chair on the front porch of the White House, everybody in the country is going to relax, breathe easy again!

HASTINGS What about the other candidates?

RAFFERTY They've erased each other. We've got a blank slate.

HASTINGS How can I expect anybody to go into a voting booth and do what I wouldn't do? I wouldn't vote for me. Not for President.

RAFFERTY You know what'll happen? Some dark horse can stampede the convention—God knows who. Maybe somebody without your integrity, somebody who wants the office for purely selfish reasons. Only one person can stop that. You.

HASTINGS Four years I'd be apologizing for getting myself stuck where I don't belong. I hate apologizers.

RAFFERTY I guess I was wrong. Go back to Wilmont, Griff. Set type. Write editorials about widening Center Street. To hell with the country.

(HASTINGS *looks distantly out the window. He seems to be thinking how much of his private life would vanish in the hot Presidential spotlight.*)

HASTINGS It's so bright up there. You can't even let your beard grow.

RAFFERTY Lincoln did.

HASTINGS I mean over a weekend.

WEBSTER There is one question we'd like to ask you, Mr. Senator. It's more or less a standard question that we ask all candidates.

HASTINGS Well?

WEBSTER Is there anything in your life that might cast reflection on the party? Or the country?

FRANCES (*Icily*) That seems a peculiar question to ask a United States Senator.

RAFFERTY You don't have to answer that, Griff.

HASTINGS Why not? I think it's a good question. I want a few minutes to think.
(RAFFERTY *gestures to* WEBSTER)

RAFFERTY We'll be out in the hall.
(RAFFERTY *and* WEBSTER *go out and close the door.* FRANCES *looks at her husband's back*)

FRANCES Griffith.

HASTINGS I've got to think, Duchess. If I only had time to sleep on it.
(FRANCES *moves a few steps toward him*)

FRANCES This is the one night in your life to stay awake, to know what's going on. You still can't see it, can you? You still don't know who wears your clothes.
(HASTINGS *takes off his coat and holds it up to her*)

HASTINGS This coat belongs to a country newspaper editor who had good enough friends to get himself elected to the United States Senate. This coat does not belong to the President of the United States.
(*He tosses the coat into a chair*)

FRANCES All my life I've been hearing that speech. Griffith, you said you didn't have any business in county politics (HASTINGS *sits down*) You said you didn't know how to be a State Legislator. You didn't think you could run the newspaper, you said the same thing about the newspaper! And see how wrong you were.

(HASTINGS *scowls*)

HASTINGS Duchess, this thing is different. A President has to be special. Everything he does and says is important. Hell, I was born unimportant. It's the only talent I've got.

FRANCES I don't believe that. Neither do you. (*Her voice softens*) The October before we were married, you and I climbed to the top of Mount Wilmont. Remember?

HASTINGS (*A short laugh*) "Mighty Mount Wilmont. Highest point in the County. One hundred ten feet above sea level."

FRANCES Up there, we looked back over the town, and I told you it was *your* town, it could be your town, and you could bid for the newspaper, and I'd help you raise the money, and we could make it the most important daily in Southeastern Ohio, and we *did! You* did! And they were good years, working together, weren't they, Griffith?

HASTINGS I had a railroad ticket in my inside coat pocket that day. You didn't know that, Duchess. I'd paid my final week's rent at the boarding house. I meant to tell you I was leaving Wilmont to take a job in a land office in Denver. But I didn't go. Because of something that happened between you and me. And it hasn't happened often enough since then, has it, Frances? (FRANCES *turns away*) You gave me the feeling I was quite a guy. Quite a guy.

35

FRANCES Griffith, I've always believed in you, now everybody else agrees with me. It's as if a door is being held open for you. Now all we have to do is walk in.

HASTINGS You make it sound like the easiest job in the world to say yes to the toughest job in the world. Well, I can't do it! I just can't do it!

FRANCES (*Growing angry*) What right do you have to say you can't do it? How can you deny the country and the friends who believe in you? And for what? For the sake of some—(*She gropes for the word*)—of some momentary appetite—

HASTINGS (*Also angry*) Get off my back, Frances.

FRANCES That's the only thing that's stopping you, isn't it? Isn't it?

HASTINGS Damn it, stop hammering at my head about that! We made a deal. We're not going to talk about it. It's over.

FRANCES If it's over, let it *be* over.
  (HASTINGS *puts on his coat*)

HASTINGS You really want this, don't you, Frances? Why?

FRANCES Not for myself. For you. It's a chance to make your life really *mean* something. But we'll forget about it. I'll never mention it again.
  (HASTINGS *is touched by his wife's emotion. He's given her a ragged time, and he knows it. He snaps his fingers nervously, wishing that this decision had fallen to somebody else, anybody else. Then, with a gambler's sudden air of recklessness, he crosses to the door and opens it.*
  RAFFERTY *and* WEBSTER *hurry in*)

RAFFERTY Well, Griff? What's the answer?

HASTINGS I'm a poker player. You deal me a royal flush, at least I'm going to pick up the cards.

(*This is a signal for jubilant action;* RAFFERTY *claps* HASTINGS *on the back,* WEBSTER *pumps his hand.* FRANCES *is silent, watching with stunned disbelief*)

RAFFERTY Great, Griff. Char-lie, get on the phone!

WEBSTER Congratulations, Senator! We'll shake up that convention!

(WEBSTER *rushes to the phone, jiggling it impatiently.* RAFFERTY *paces, waving his hands, the general before the battle*)

WEBSTER Operator! Operator, find me the head sign painter at the Coliseum! I don't care if you have to get him out of bed. What the hell is that Philadelphia number?

RAFFERTY Gotta get Doc and the Judge back here; dig up some public stenographers, and a platoon of bellboys.

(DOC *and the* JUDGE *burst into the room, excitedly*)

DOC Walt, what the hell has happened?

WEBSTER Plenty!

DOC It's all over the hotel that Higgy made a deal.

RAFFERTY Not with us.

(TAD *enters, followed by* HIGGY)

TAD Higgy's picked up enough votes to kill your chances dead, Charlie.

HIGGY Charles, out of Christian charity, I've come back to offer your poor disappointed Governor the Vice-Presidency.

37

WEBSTER That's very interesting, Higgy. You're just in time. (*To* HASTINGS) Senator, this is the Honorable James J. Higgins of New Jersey

RAFFERTY Higgy, I'd like you to shake hands with our party's nominee—and the next President of the United States: Griffith Pericles Hastings.

(HIGGY *glances toward* HASTINGS *with disbelief and pained indignation. The smart operator has just outsmarted himself.* HASTINGS, *with an air of genuine grandeur, extends his hand to the dumfounded* HIGGY)

The Lights Fade

(*In the darkness we hear the tumult of voices echoing in the convention hall. Again and again the gavel pounds*)

CHAIRMAN'S VOICE (*Booming*) Illinois yields the floor to the delegation from the State of Massachusetts.

(*There is a crest of excited reaction*)

WEBSTER'S VOICE The Great Commonwealth of Massachusetts wishes to change its vote and casts a unanimous ballot for the distinguished Senator from the Buckeye State—Griffith P. Hastings!

(*The cheers are deafening. There is a wild, impromptu chorus of "Beautiful Ohio," which fades away into awed silence. Projections of Washington's Monument and the Capitol dome appear impressionistically on the cyclorama*)

HASTINGS' VOICE I do solemnly swear.

JUSTICE'S VOICE That I will faithfully execute.

HASTINGS' VOICE That I will faithfully execute.

JUSTICE'S VOICE The office of the President of the United States.

HASTINGS' VOICE   The office of the President of the United States.

JUSTICE'S VOICE   And will, to the best of my ability—

HASTINGS' VOICE   And will, to the best of my ability—

JUSTICE'S VOICE   Preserve, protect, and defend the Constitution of the United States.

HASTINGS' VOICE   Preserve, protect, and defend the Constitution of the United States.

JUSTICE'S VOICE   So help me God.
   (*Pause*)

HASTINGS' VOICE (*Softly*)   So help me God!
   (*The music strikes in with "Hail to the Chief," full at first, then fading to background*)

SCENE 2

Scene: The upstairs sitting room of the Presidential apart-
ment in the White House. March 4 of the following year. It is
midafternoon. In the distance, we still hear the military band
playing "Hail to the Chief." There are two medium-sized
packing cases on the floor. There are tall doors downstage right
and left; the right ones lead to the corridors of the White
House, the left ones to other rooms of the private suite. Near
the door downstage right is a panel of buzzers. COBB, *the Chief*
Steward, enters. He is dignified, graying, immaculately dressed.
He has none of the mannerisms of a butler, more those of a
diplomat. FRANCES *follows him, wearing a long fur cape, a*
flowered hat, and carrying a muff. She is tremendously im-
pressed, but is trying to conceal it.

COBB This is the Executive Suite, Mrs. Hastings. I hope you'll
find it comfortable. Your private rooms are through here.
(*He calls off*) Don't let the van leave. Here are some more
boxes to go.

FRANCES These are *my* packages. The President's.
    (COBB *crosses and presses one of the buttons on the panel*)

COBB I'll have them opened immediately.
    (*A* MAID *enters.* COBB *indicates the boxes, which she starts*
    to open. From off, there is a flurry of activity—voices and
    applause)

FRANCES The President's coming. Hurry. May I call on you for anything we may need?

COBB You can summon me, or anyone in the household, by using these buzzers.

FRANCES Thank you. Will you tell all your people, please, that we have only one task, really. To make certain the President is comfortable here.

COBB Yes, Mrs. Hastings.

(*The* MAID *unwraps an ornate footstool*)

FRANCES *(To* COBB*)* Put it right here. It's my husband's favorite stool. He loves to rest his feet on it. I made the petit point myself. (*Indicating the other boxes*) I'll take care of those.

(*The* MAID *exits.* COBB *crosses downstage right to entrance*)

COBB *(Calling offstage)* Right in here, Mr. President.

(HASTINGS *enters. He is wearing a swallowtail coat, striped pants, and he carries a silk top hat and a black topcoat. The ride up Pennsylvania Avenue, the brisk March air, the stimulus of the cheers and applause seem to have had an almost chemical effect on* HASTINGS. *His cheeks are glowing, his eyes brighter; he actually seems taller than before.* COBB *nods, then goes out, to leave the new* PRESIDENT *and* FIRST LADY *alone for the first time*)

HASTINGS *(Over his shoulder to* COBB, *tardily, preoccupied)* Oh, thank you. Thank you. (FRANCES *opens her mouth to speak, but stops, realizing that her husband is in a kind of baffled and wondering reverie. Slowly he walks around the room. He looks at the Great Seal of the United States, embossed on the back of a chair center stage. He touches it tentatively, as if it might break or vanish.* FRANCES *is silent, sensing that this is a thunderous moment in her husband's life*) Frances, we're going to live here. Those people today, along the streets cheering, they want me, Frances. They really want me. I don't know why they voted for me. I wonder if *they* know. But I'm going to do a job for them. (*He places his hat and coat on couch*) I'm not scared anymore. I'm not even worried. Well, I'm a little worried. But it's going to be fine. Everything's going to be fine.

FRANCES   And your address was splendid, Mr. President.

HASTINGS   (*With a little laugh*)   When I was a Senator, it would just have been a speech. Now it's an address. (*He has crossed and embraced her*) Damn, my feet hurt. During that parade I thought they were going to make me stand the whole four years. (*He sits on the couch and takes off one shoe. His eyes light on the footstool*) Oh my God, Frances, look what they've got here. A monstrosity just like you knitted for me back home.

(COBB *enters in time to overhear this.* FRANCES, *embarrassed, moves upstage*)

COBB   Mr. President, may I welcome you on behalf of the housekeeping staff. My name is Cobb. I'm the Chief Steward.

HASTINGS   (*Making the name stick*)   Cobb. C-o-b-b. I've met so many people today, I've been using an old politician's trick: when somebody tells you who he is, you write his name across his forehead. (*With a grin*) Cobb, you might ask the people around here not to wash their faces for a few days.

(HASTINGS *laughs.* COBB *smiles, and picks up* HASTINGS' *hat and coat from the couch*)

COBB   Sir, a member of the interim office staff is standing by with the schedule for the rest of the day.

HASTINGS   (*Rubbing his foot*)   Fine. Fine. Send him in. Let's get it over with.

COBB Yes, sir.

> (COBB *goes out.* FRANCES *begins pacing, casting sidelong glances at her husband's shoeless foot*)

FRANCES Griffith, these people are really seeing you for the first time, aren't they? Later on, I think it would be nice if you "unbend" a little. But this first day is so important. Just remember who you are. That's all I ask.

HASTINGS (*Writing on his own forehead*) Look. "John Quincy Adams." (*Knock at door.* HASTINGS *puts on shoe and begins lacing it up*) Come in.

> (BRUCE BELLINGHAM *enters. There is a quiet confidence about him. He is in his mid-thirties, good-looking, and wouldn't be caught dead wearing his Phi Beta Kappa key.* BELLINGHAM *has several pages of typed memoranda and a telegram in his hand*)

BELLINGHAM Mrs. Hastings, Mr. President. May I submit today's calendar? And I knew you'd want to see this telegram at once.

HASTINGS (*Taking the telegram*) Now wait a minute. Who are you?

BELLINGHAM I'm sorry. I should have introduced myself. My name is Bellingham.

HASTINGS Bellingham.

BELLINGHAM I'm part of the inter-administration liaison staff.

HASTINGS Every four or eight years, you get four to eight days' work—that the idea? (BELLINGHAM *nods.* HASTINGS *smiles*) Not what I'd call a steady job.

BELLINGHAM Just a short strip of adhesive tape between ad-ministrations.

(*Both men laugh*)

HASTINGS (*Scanning the telegram*) Damn.

FRANCES Is anything wrong, dear?

HASTINGS (*Folding the wire and stuffing it in his vest pocket*) Nothing. (*To* BELLINGHAM) O.K. Roll out the schedule.

BELLINGHAM Four-thirty—tea for the Inaugural party; Five-fifteen—reception for the Supreme Court Justices and the senior members of Congress; Six—reception for the Diplo-matic Corps; Six-forty-five—international press representa-tives; Seven—greetings to the White House staff—that can be very brief; Seven-oh-five—leave for the Inauguration Banquet; Eight-twenty-five—dessert at the second Inaugura-tion Banquet at the Willard.

HASTINGS (*Wryly*) Eight-forty-five—leave for Ford's Theatre.

FRANCES (*Reaching for the paper*) Why not let me handle the schedule?

HASTINGS (*Taking the memorandum from her*) Don't try to drive the flivver, Duchess. (*To* BELLINGHAM) Just keep me headed in the right direction and I'll be there.

BELLINGHAM Mr. Arthur Anderson has asked to see you as soon as possible, privately.

HASTINGS Fine. Make it early next week.

BELLINGHAM He's waiting outside, sir.

HASTINGS Oh? I guess you'd better send him in.

BELLINGHAM Yes, sir.

(BELLINGHAM *goes out.* HASTINGS *turns to* FRANCES, *worried*)

HASTINGS I figured Anderson was one Cabinet post we had all locked up. (*Knock*) Come in.
> (ANDERSON *enters, carrying a brief case. He is proper, stiff, incapable of informality of any kind. Brilliant without being witty, dignified without real warmth, even his good manners cannot wholly conceal his contempt for ineptitude*)

ANDERSON Mr. President, please forgive my intrusion.

HASTINGS (*Crosses to shake hands with him*) Glad to see you, Mr. Secretary. You know my wife?

ANDERSON I have already had the honor.

HASTINGS Sit down, Mr. Secretary.

ANDERSON I'll be as brief as possible. Sir, we are confronted with an urgent foreign policy decision.
> (*He sits on the couch.* FRANCES *crosses upstage right to the table, and starts removing the contents of the last box. She cannot avoid eavesdropping when such important matters are at stake*)

HASTINGS (*Sitting*) You didn't waste much time getting your feet wet in the State Department mud puddle, did you?

ANDERSON I came down right after the first of the year for a briefing. This morning, the American Ambassador in Tokyo was handed a communication which calls for an entirely new policy on the Mandated Islands.

HASTINGS The Mandated Islands.

ANDERSON Our treaty commitments do not make it clear whether an island under mandate is, in fact, under military protectorate.

HASTINGS Yes. You know, in the Senate I was mainly concerned with domestic issues. Now let's cut this right down to the bone; what's the gist of the problem, as you see it?

ANDERSON This new challenge makes it imperative that we issue an immediate and definitive declaration of the American position.

HASTINGS Well, what do you think, Mr. Secretary?

ANDERSON To me, a mandate is meaningless unless it is implemented. The issue is the extent of the implementation.

HASTINGS If that's how you feel, I want you to know I'm one hundred per cent behind you. Go ahead and make a statement.

ANDERSON Mr. President, the decision should be yours.

HASTINGS (*Taking a deep breath*) Well, here's what we'll do. We'll get a committee to make a study of the whole picture.

ANDERSON There have been two reports by previous bipartisan committees.

HASTINGS Oh? What'd they say?

ANDERSON The two committees were diametrically opposed. (*He removes the two hefty reports from his brief case*)

HASTINGS Tell me, Mr. Anderson. Arthur. What's the *right* thing to do?

ANDERSON My recommendation would, I am afraid, run directly counter to the promises made during the recent campaign. (*A pause*)

HASTINGS What would happen if we didn't do anything?

ANDERSON I don't know, sir.

HASTINGS Well, leave it with me. The basic stuff. I'll get back to you as soon as I can.
(ANDERSON *hands him the two thick reports*)

HASTINGS Don't they have a digest, a condensation of these things?

ANDERSON These *are* the condensations, Mr. President.
(HASTINGS *nods*)

HASTINGS Fine. Fine. Thank you.
(ANDERSON *starts out*)

ANDERSON I'll be waiting for your decision, sir.

HASTINGS Good. Thank you. Fine.

ANDERSON (*Nodding a good-by*) Mrs. Hastings.
(*He goes out*)

HASTINGS (*Troubled*) I'm off to a great start.

FRANCES (*Reasonably*) Griffith, you can't be expected to be an authority on all these matters. So you have assistants who are knowledgeable. Like Mr. Anderson. Or anybody else you choose.

HASTINGS If I can understand them.

FRANCES At the newspaper, did you set all the type yourself? In the Senate, did you read every word in the Congressional Record? Of course you didn't. Nobody does. (*Touching his arm reassuringly*) Griffith, a great many people are going to help you. We're all going to help you.
(FRANCES *goes off toward the private rooms of the suite. The new President leafs through the reports, scowling.*

He is a painfully slow reader, and digesting a typewritten page is an agony for him. BELLINGHAM *re-enters with a sizable stack of mail*)

BELLINGHAM Here's the important mail, sir. The wires and cablegrams are on top. We've screened out the purely congratulatory stuff.

(HASTINGS *takes the correspondence, glances at it, then transfers it to the desk, where an impressive mountain of reading matter is piling up*)

HASTINGS Thank you, thank you, Mr. Bellingham. I'll get right at it, as soon as—(*He looks at the schedule on desk*) Tell me, where's this "Tea for the Inaugural party"? It's past four-thirty.

BELLINGHAM That's going on right now, in the East Room. (FRANCES *comes back in*)

HASTINGS Is that where the boys are? Down there with all that marble, drinking tea? Why don't we ask 'em up here?

BELLINGHAM It's a party of several hundred people.

HASTINGS Not everybody. Just a few close friends.

FRANCES Don't you want a little rest, Griffith?

HASTINGS Rest, hell. I want to see somebody I can talk to. (*To* BELLINGHAM) You know Senator Loomis? On sight?

BELLINGHAM Yes, sir.

HASTINGS Ask him to get some of the boys together—Walt, and Ax, and the Judge. Have 'em bring their teacups up here.

(BELLINGHAM *nods and starts out*)

HASTINGS One other thing—

BELLINGHAM Yes, Mr. President?

HASTINGS (*Crossing to him*) Does "tea" mean . . . tea?

BELLINGHAM (*After a slight hesitation*) Whatever refreshments are required can probably be made available.

HASTINGS (*Measuring him*) Maybe you ought to stay longer than four days. (*Abruptly*) Just a minute. What does— (*He breaks off, digs the folded telegram out of his pocket and studies it*) What exactly does "quid pro quo" mean?

BELLINGHAM It means a horse trade, Mr. President. I scratch your back, you scratch mine.

HASTINGS That's what I thought. (*Looking at wire*) Why the hell doesn't he say that? You got any plans after this "interim" business?

BELLINGHAM Well, I'm on a loan from the Commerce Department. I'm a consultant over there. It's Civil Service, purely nonpolitical.

HASTINGS If I can make an arrangement with your boss, would you consider coming over here? Wouldn't be Civil Service, of course. (BELLINGHAM *is too Washington-wise to turn handsprings at the suggestion of a Presidential appointment*) Think about it.

BELLINGHAM I will, sir.
(*He goes out respectfully.* FRANCES *has been simmering with pent-up comment*)

FRANCES Griffith, are you sending that young man, whom you have only just met, to obtain illegal beverages?
(HASTINGS *isn't listening; he re-examines the telegram*)

HASTINGS I need a drink. And I think you could use one, too, Duchess.

(*He kicks the footstool under the chair, then sits*)

FRANCES As First Lady, I think I should abstain.

HASTINGS Swell. You can abstain for both of us.
(*He puzzles over the telegram*)

FRANCES (*Crossing toward him*) You want to tell me who the telegram's from?

HASTINGS Samuel Cavendish.

FRANCES And he's turned down the Cabinet appointment.

HASTINGS (*Hands her the telegram*) No, damn it. He's accepted. How do you talk to a man who's worth eight hundred million dollars? What do I call him? "Sam"? I promised Treasury to Josh Loomis.

FRANCES Well, just be glad you won't have anyone like Mr. Loomis in your Cabinet.
(*She puts telegram on table*)

HASTINGS (*Irked*) *Senator* Loomis.

FRANCES Why don't you give a Cabinet post to that young man you've known nearly five minutes—Mr. Bellingham?

HASTINGS What's wrong with him?

FRANCES Perhaps nothing. But you don't know a thing about him. You've got to be more cautious now, Griffith.

HASTINGS I like him! I happen to like him! That's the way I work. That's the way I am. You're not going to change me now.

(COBB *enters with the tea wagon. There are two bottles of bourbon on the bottom shelf of the cart*)

HASTINGS (*Following* COBB *and the tea cart*) Medicinal?

COBB *Bonded* medicinal.
(*Disapprovingly,* FRANCES *starts off left*)

FRANCES I'll be in here dressing, if you need me.
(*She goes out, but* HASTINGS *doesn't realize she's gone*)

HASTINGS You don't have to stay, Cobb. This bunch knows how to get a cork out of a bottle.
(*He chortles amiably*)

COBB Yes, Mr. President.
(COBB *leaves discreetly.* HASTINGS *pours himself a short drink and downs it, straight. Braced, he looks around the room, realizing for the first time that he is alone. He tries to fight off the feeling of fright at the pinnacle on which he finds himself*)

HASTINGS Frances? (*He is very much alone, cut off. He crosses to the hallway door. It is almost a moment of panic*) Fellas? Where is everybody?
(*He notices the whisky bottle and glass where he left them on the desk. He crosses quickly, picks them up, and with the sleeve of his morning coat he wipes off the circle left by the moist glass. He stands, miserable, like an unwelcome guest in his own house*)

LOOMIS' VOICE (*From the hallway*) I guess we're supposed to go right on in.
(*With relief,* HASTINGS *crosses to greet* LOOMIS, *who enters, carrying a teacup in one hand*)

HASTINGS Josh!

LOOMIS Now this is what I call a real special privilege. Congratulations, Mr. President.
(*They shake hands warmly*)

HASTINGS Thanks, amigo. (RAFFERTY, WEBSTER, *and* DOC *enter. They are subdued and impressed by the occasion and the surroundings.* HASTINGS *makes an extra effort to make them feel comfortable*) Come on in, fellas. I've been waiting for you. (*There seems to be a new barrier of formality between the* GANG *and* HASTINGS. *Each waits for the* PRESIDENT *to speak first*) Walt! Did you ever think we'd make it?

RAFFERTY It's a great day, Mr. President.

(HASTINGS *claps* RAFFERTY *on the shoulder, then extends his hand to* DOC *and* WEBSTER)

HASTINGS Charlie. Doc.

WEBSTER Mr. President.

DOC (*with an inclination of his head, almost as if to royalty*) Mr. President. (JUDGE CORRIGLIONE *appears in the doorway, and stops, genuinely awed.* HASTINGS *calls to him*) Come on in, Judge. Pull up a bench.

CORRIGLIONE (*Coming in*) I hope we aren't imposing on you, Mr. President.

HASTINGS Imposing! I invited you up here, didn't I? (*Addressing them all*) Starting now, let's forget this "Mr. President" stuff. I've been "Griff" all these years, don't put any "Misters" between us, now. (*In the doorway, he spots a short, bubbly little man whose face has the mobility of a clown's, and who darts about with almost annoying good spirits. This is* AXEL MALEY. *The* PRESIDENT *shouts a greeting to him*) Ax! Join the party. But if you call me "Mr. President", I'll kick you right back into the middle of Ohio!

(MALEY *hesitates. Then he decides to take a chance and his face lights up*)

53

MALEY Hi ya, Prez.
(*Everybody laughs*)

HASTINGS What do you think of the White House, Ax?

MALEY It's got the Wilmont County Courthouse beat all hollow. And say, you even made the front page of your own newspaper.
(*There is more laughter at this, and the stiffness begins to subside*)

HASTINGS (*Clapping him on the shoulder*) Damn it, Ax, it's good to see you. I wasn't sure I could laugh in this suit of clothes! (*Crossing to the tea cart*) Now. What'll you have?

WEBSTER Tea, I suppose.
(*Slyly,* HASTINGS *pulls out two bottles from beneath the tea cart*)

HASTINGS I don't imagine anybody's interested in bourbon?
(*There is hearty approval.* MALEY *waltzes to the* PRESIDENT'S *side, putting his teacup daintily on the cart*)

MALEY No sugar in mine, please!
(*Everybody laughs.* HASTINGS *pours.* CORRIGLIONE *has not offered his teacup;* HASTINGS *smiles at him warmly*)

HASTINGS Come on, Judge. None of this gang is going to report you to the Bar Association)

CORRIGLIONE (*Crossing*) Well, all right. A short one. Thank you, Mr. President.

MALEY (*Lifting his cup*) Gentlemen. To them as is in and them as is out. Especially us as is in.
(*Everybody laughs and starts to toast. But* RAFFERTY *halts them*)

RAFFERTY   No. Wait a minute. (*He looks around the room at each face with that sense of drama he used so well in the smoke-filled room*) I want to propose a toast. To the only man in this room. (*Facing* HASTINGS) Because all of us here are just extensions of you, Griff. Extra eyes, extra minds, extra hands. Any time you need us in the next four years—

WEBSTER   Eight years, Walt! Eight!
   (*The others affirm this.*)

RAFFERTY   Any time in the bright and glorious years ahead—
(RAFFERTY *moves deliberately to the panel of buzzers*) Whenever you need any of us, we'll be a finger tip away. (*Indicating the buzzers, as if each were marked*) Doc. Charlie. Josh. The Judge. Axel Maley, Esquire. (*Pointing to the bottom button*) Your humble servant, Walter Rafferty. (*He lifts his cup in a toast*) Gentlemen. The President of the United States.

GANG   The President.
   (*They drink. It is a solemn moment*)

HASTINGS   (*Moved*)   Thank you, boys. I didn't expect to feel this good today. I don't know whether it's the words or the schnapps!
   (FRANCES *enters in her Inauguration gown*)

RAFFERTY   Why, Frances, what a beautiful gown.
   (*They all turn to look at her*)

HASTINGS   Look what can happen to a country editor these days; winds up married to the First Lady.

FRANCES   (*A little embarrassed at the attention*)   Do you like the material?

HASTINGS   I'd better like it. For what that cost, we could've bought a used linotype machine! You'll wear it once and they'll stick it in the Smithsonian. Sit down, fellas, sit down. (*They begin to make themselves more comfortable.* LOOMIS *settles easily onto the sofa center stage*)

MALEY What you worrying about money for, Prez? (*He indicates* LOOMIS *with his cup*) Just have your Secretary of the Treasury here print you up a bushel-basketful of thousand-dollar bills.
(*Everybody chuckles at this, except* HASTINGS)

HASTINGS (*Pained*) Josh, a hell of a thing has happened. I feel terrible about it.

RAFFERTY What?
(*The* PRESIDENT *turns to his campaign manager with irritation*)

HASTINGS I thought we had these Cabinet appointments all nailed down. And Josh was supposed to be my Secretary of Treasury.

RAFFERTY (*Blandly*) That's right. As soon as your Senate buddies say O.K.

HASTINGS Well, look at this wire. (*Handing him the telegram*) Cavendish accepted. You told me this was just a gesture because he plunked a hundred thousand into the campaign kitty. Do you expect me to pitch an old friend like Josh in the ash can, just to pay off a campaign debt? (RAFFERTY *is thoughtful*)

RAFFERTY Let me see that Cabinet list.

HASTINGS Here. (*He fishes a sheet of paper from an inside pocket, then turns to* LOOMIS) I don't know what to say, Josh. I'm embarrassed.

LOOMIS Naturally I'm disappointed, amigo, but Cavendish is one of the smartest men in the country. He'd have to be to pile up all that money.

HASTINGS How'm I going to do this job with a bunch of walking bankbooks and carnation-wearing diplomats?

FRANCES You promised to surround yourself with the best minds.

HASTINGS Aren't there any good minds who also know how to speak Ohio? My friends happen to be worthy and bright. Am I supposed to say: "Thank you, good-by, go home"?

RAFFERTY None of us did what we did because we expected anything out of it.

HASTINGS I want the Cabinet *I* want. Not what somebody thinks would look good in a history book.

RAFFERTY (*Drawing out a pencil*) Well, maybe we can do a little juggling.

FRANCES Griffith, why don't you save these decisions for a regular business day when there aren't so many pressures. Now I think our schedule calls for us to be—
    (RAFFERTY *scribbles something on the list and hands it back to* HASTINGS)

HASTINGS Can we make this change?

RAFFERTY (*Nods*) I'll fix it so there aren't any ruffled feelings.

HASTINGS (*Enthusiastically*) Now you're talking. Everybody, meet my Secretary of Interior! What about it, Josh?

LOOMIS (*With a modest laugh*) What can I do? I've been drafted.

VOICES Congratulations, Mr. Secretary. Good luck, Josh. Take good care of Interior.

HASTINGS Hell, we'll get all the good poker players away from the Senate. Better watch out, Walt, we'll take all your money.

RAFFERTY I'm out of the picture. Tomorrow morning I'll be on a train to Columbus.

HASTINGS (*Shocked*) What's that?

RAFFERTY I'm going back home. I've got a law practice to take care of.

HASTINGS But you're my Postmaster General.

RAFFERTY What do I know about stamps? I'm a lawyer.

HASTINGS I thought it was all settled.

RAFFERTY I said I'd consider it. I didn't say I'd accept it.

HASTINGS You just told me that any time I needed you—

RAFFERTY Pick up a phone. I can be here overnight. The trains are still running.

HASTINGS (*Pleading*) You can't leave me, Walt.

RAFFERTY A hundred other guys are better qualified for Postmaster General.

HASTINGS You've got to stay right here in Washington.

RAFFERTY Doing what?
    (HASTINGS *fishes into his pocket for the Cabinet list and examines it again*)

HASTINGS We're not really committed on the Justice Department, are we?

RAFFERTY No.

HASTINGS That's where I want you, Walt. As my Attorney General.

RAFFERTY That's a tremendous responsibility, Griff.

HASTINGS You can handle it. My God, you did a brilliant job on the campaign. You've got to stay. I need you.
(*Pause. Everything is going precisely as engineered, but* RAFFERTY *and his cohorts are playing it with skillful innocence*)

RAFFERTY Well, I'm a poker player, too. I'll play whatever cards you deal me.

HASTINGS (*Shakes* RAFFERTY's *hand warmly*) Thank you, Walt. (*Pacing up and down*) Well, it's not gonna be so lonesome around here, Duchess. Say, what about Charlie?

WEBSTER (*Hastily*) Oh, Walt's already suggested me for a little job at the Veterans' Bureau. I'll just be off in a corner some place, doing my job.

HASTINGS And we're not going to leave the Honorable Axel Maley out in the cold, are we?

MALEY Don't worry, Prez. As long as Walt's got a warm office, *I* won't freeze.
(BELLINGHAM *enters, pauses at the door*)

BELLINGHAM Excuse me, Mr. President, the Supreme Court Justices are beginning to arrive.

DOC Any Supreme Court Justices in here?

MALEY Dog-gone, I forgot my robes!
(HASTINGS *goes quickly behind the desk*)

HASTINGS Just a minute, I want to make some changes in this Cabinet list. (*Glancing up*) Say, I want you boys all to meet

Mr. Bellingham. He may be working with us. Ax, pour him a little orange pekoe.

MALEY   Tea, Mr. Bellingham?

BELLINGHAM   Thank you.

MALEY   (*Crossing to the tea cart*)   You do? Around here, if you really want tea, you'd better ask for bourbon.
(HASTINGS *has been searching the drawers of the desk, looking for a pencil. Suddenly he stops*)

HASTINGS   (*Soberly*)   Say, look what I found. (*He holds up a half-empty bottle of ink-like medicine*) I guess it belongs to my honorable predecessor.
(BELLINGHAM *crosses to* HASTINGS)

BELLINGHAM   I'll see that it's forwarded to him.
(*But* HASTINGS *is still studying the bottle*)

HASTINGS   I knew the man was sick, but when I sat beside him in that limousine, all the way down Pennsylvania Avenue—God that was a long trip!—he didn't say a word. It was like riding in a hearse beside the body. (*He unscrews the cap and tastes the medicine from his finger tip. It's bitter*) Is this stuff "President Juice"? The poor bastard.
(COBB *enters*)

COBB   Excuse me, Mr. President, the Supreme Court Justices are all here.

RAFFERTY   Come on, boys, we'd better go.
(*The* GANG *moves to leave, but* HASTINGS *speaks quickly, to stop them*)

HASTINGS   Wait a minute. This is the first time I'm really going out there on my own. Not just waving, I mean, or reading off a paper. The parade's over. Now I've got to start waiting on the customers. (*Simply*) If any of you say prayers, or have friends who know how to say prayers, ask them to mention me a couple of times, just in passing. I'll be grateful.

RAFFERTY Sure, Griff.

CORRIGLIONE (*Genuinely*) I'll light a candle for you, Mr. President.

HASTINGS Thanks, Judge. I'll need it. (*Now he is the bluff "good fellow" again,*) See? Nothing to worry about. Not a damn thing to worry about. Because I've got my friends with me! Thanks for coming, boys. Remember, the key's always under the front mat. Of course, there may be a dozen Secret Service men standing on it.

(*Laughing,* DOC, LOOMIS, WEBSTER, CORRIGLIONE, *and* RAFFERTY *go out.* MALEY *steps to the doorway*)

MALEY (*Winking at the* PRESIDENT, *as he leaves*) Say, if you ever get a parking ticket in this town, I know the Chief of Police. See you, Prez.

(*The* PRESIDENT *chuckles as* MALEY *leaves*)

BELLINGHAM Excuse me, sir, but we can't get too far behind schedule.

HASTINGS Mr. Bellingham, I want to announce a couple more Cabinet appointments. Today.

FRANCES (*Concerned*) Griffith—

HASTINGS What's the protocol? Can I release them straight to the press, or does the Senate want the news ahead of the newspapers?

BELLINGHAM The releases can be concurrent.

HASTINGS Fine. I've persuaded Walt Rafferty to accept the Attorney Generalship. And Senator Loomis will head up the Department of Interior.

(FRANCES *is determined to stop her husband's rashness*)

FRANCES Mr. Bellingham, the President will send you a written memorandum when and if he decides—

HASTINGS (*Lashing out*) Frances, I don't know what language you speak. But I just said, in English, that Walt Rafferty and Josh Loomis are going to be in my Cabinet! For the sweet love of God, will you try to be on my side? (*Pause.* BELLINGHAM *is embarrassed to be present at this domestic squabbling. The* PRESIDENT *softens*) Duchess, we've got to spend four years in this place. Together. Let's try to put on a decent show for the people.

FRANCES (*With her eyes lowered she crosses to the doorway*) Whatever you say, Griffith. I'll be waiting for you out in the hallway.

(*She goes out*)

BELLINGHAM (*Clearing his throat*) Is that all, Mr. President?

HASTINGS Just see to it the new Cabinet nominations are in the papers tonight.

BELLINGHAM (*Picking up his brief case*) I'll send out the press release immediately, and prepare the necessary papers to go up to the Hill.

HASTINGS Good. Thank you.

BELLINGHAM Any further details can be handled by my successor.

HASTINGS Your successor! I want you to stay.

(*There is a pause.* BELLINGHAM *wets his lips, and looks squarely at* HASTINGS)

BELLINGHAM I'm sorry, sir. I can't.

HASTINGS Why not? Don't you approve of my friends? O.K. they're not Princeton professors. But they're good guys. You'll get on with them. Or maybe you're on the other side of the political fence.

BELLINGHAM I voted for you, sir. I live over in Arlington, where they let people vote.

HASTINGS Then you're going to stay.

BELLINGHAM (*With polite evasion*) The Justices are waiting for you, Mr. President.

HASTINGS (*Angrily*) O.K., Mr. Interim! You can strap up your fancy brief case and leave any time you want to. I don't know anything about you anyhow. Hell, there's ten thousand like you in Washington.

BELLINGHAM Yes, sir. (*He starts out*)

HASTINGS Bellingham.

(BELLINGHAM *turns.* HASTINGS *studies him. He wants this man. He respects him, and needs him. It will be a major personal victory if he can persuade* BELLINGHAM *to stay*)

HASTINGS (*Slowly*) Take your pick. You can go back to the Commerce Department and write memos nobody reads. Or you can stay here, and help me do a job. Help me *try* to do a job.

(BELLINGHAM *is wavering.* RAFFERTY *comes into the room*)

RAFFERTY Hey, I've got nine beards down in the Oval Room. They're getting a little restless!

(RAFFERTY *looks from the* PRESIDENT *to* BELLINGHAM. *The younger man stares at the old political hand, whose cocksure attitude says: "I own the White House"*)

BELLINGHAM   I'll stay, Mr. President.

HASTINGS   Good! (HASTINGS *crosses to* BELLINGHAM) Say, what's your first name?

BELLINGHAM   Bruce.

HASTINGS   Bruce, shake hands with Walt. You're on the same team!
(BELLINGHAM *and* RAFFERTY *look at each other. They do not shake hands.* HASTINGS *goes back to the desk and picks up* ANDERSON's *heavy digests. He crosses back to the two men.* RAFFERTY *reaches out his hand to take the books, but the* PRESIDENT *gives them to* BELLINGHAM)

HASTINGS   Say, will you read through these things and tell me what to do?
(*Taking a deep breath, the* PRESIDENT *strides out.* RAFFERTY *and* BELLINGHAM *stand facing each other, not moving. The air between them has a warmth approaching Absolute Zero*)

The Curtain Falls

ACT TWO

SCENE I

Scene: The basement of a house on L Street in Washington. Six months later. This is a poker-game room, which is mostly below ground level of a rather musty old Victorian house. Through the dormer windows, high in the room, we see the looming presence of the Capitol dome, ablaze with light. At stage right, descending directly toward the audience, is a staircase, which is outside the room itself. At the foot of the stairs is the only entrance to the room—a heavily bolted door. It is after midnight on a mild September night. There is a large circular poker table downstage center, with appropriate green felt. An overhead fixture casts a tight circle of light around the players. Downstage right is a side table loaded with glasses, ice buckets, mixers, and fifths of bourbon, Scotch, and rye. Downstage left is an overstuffed chair. The JUDGE is sitting on the arm, away from the poker party, leafing through a blue-backed legal document. His place at the table is vacant. At back, in the shadows, is a scarred upright piano. Five men sit around the table, intent on their cards. The players are RAFFERTY, MALEY, WEBSTER, DOC, and LOOMIS. All are in shirt sleeves except DOC, who wears a brigadier general's uniform. They are deep in the end-game of a hand of draw poker.

LOOMIS (*Shoving forward a stack of chips*) Ten and raise you ten.

WEBSTER Ten and ten better.

LOOMIS   What if Griff doesn't come tonight?

RAFFERTY   He'll be here.
(DOC *looks at his cards with disgust and tosses them down.
He rises from the table and crosses toward the liquor*)

MALEY   Why don't you take off your coat, Doc?

DOC   It's against Army regulations.

LOOMIS   That's for colonels on down, boy. Show me where
it says in the manual that a brigadier general can't play
poker in his shirt sleeves.

MALEY   He's just jealous, Doc, 'cause they didn't give him no
uniform over at Interior. (*Smirking*) But I'll tell you who
really got gypped! Poor old Walt! All those policemen under
him, and the whole FBI, and they don't even give him a
badge!

RAFFERTY   Play cards, Ax.

MALEY   Oh, sure, sure. I stay. I always stay.
(RAFFERTY *glances thoughtfully toward* CORRIGLIONE, *then
turns his attention back to his own cards.* LOOMIS *and*
RAFFERTY *measure each other across the table*)

WEBSTER   (*Laying down his cards*) Two pair, ten high.

RAFFERTY   Three jacks.
(RAFFERTY *takes in the pot*)

WEBSTER   Do you realize that's a week's salary for the head of
the Veterans' Bureau?

LOOMIS   I ache for you, boy.

RAFFERTY   Shall we deal you in this time, Judge?

CORRIGLIONE   Not yet.

RAFFERTY Speed it up, will you? We want that ready for Griff to sign when he gets here.

LOOMIS How about you, Doc? You in?
   (DOC *nods affirmatively*)

MALEY If I was the President's personal physician, like certain people in this room, I'd prescribe a few hands of draw every night.

DOC Same prescription I give myself. Not my fault if he won't take the medicine.

LOOMIS I'll tell you what's wrong with Griff: he's got a severe case of Frances Greeley Hastings. (*Shaking his head*) With half the country female—and some of 'em even pretty—he had to marry the Duchess!

RAFFERTY What makes you an authority on marriage?

LOOMIS Being a bachelor, I know everything about it. A fella on a river bank has a better seat for a drowning than the boy out there in the water going under.

DOC (*Snorts*) Washington is full of great men, and the women they married when they were very young.
   (*He sits at the poker table*)

LOOMIS Anybody got jacks or better?

WEBSTER I'll open.
   (*He tosses in a chip*)

LOOMIS Cards, gents?

MALEY I got a great hand here. But if nobody minds, I'd like four new cards.
   (LOOMIS *deals four cards to* MALEY, *who lets out a gurgle of delight as he picks up each one*)

67

MALEY Oh! Well! How about this! My, my, my! (*He tosses in his cards*) I'm out!

>   (RAFFERTY *cuts the deck, but holds the second half of it in mid-air as he sees the* JUDGE *coming toward the table. All attention turns to the* JUDGE)

CORRIGLIONE (*Tossing the legal document onto the table in front of* RAFFERTY) I never saw that. I didn't read it.

RAFFERTY All right. You didn't read it. What do you think of it?

>   (*Pause.* CORRIGLIONE *doesn't answer*)

LOOMIS Is it legal?

CORRIGLIONE If you can get the President to sign it, it's legal. Declare war, and murder is legal. (CORRIGLIONE *puts his hand on* RAFFERTY'S *shoulder*) Walt. Why don't you hold up a bank? A nice, clean, straightforward felony, with a gun in your hand.

RAFFERTY Is that humor, Your Honor?

CORRIGLIONE I've gone along on a lot of things, you know that. But this one scares me.

RAFFERTY Why?

CORRIGLIONE How can you justify signing these oil reserves over to Interior?

RAFFERTY Who's going to ask a question like that?

CORRIGLIONE A grand jury. A Congressional Committee. Anybody who suspects malfeasance.

RAFFERTY There isn't going to be any malfeasance.

CORRIGLIONE Then what do you want this executive order for?

RAFFERTY What do you care, Judge? You never read it.

CORRIGLIONE Why do you keep asking me to these parties?
(*He turns to get his hat and brief case*)

DOC You're a helluva poker player.

LOOMIS Sit down, Corriglione. We'll deal you in.

CORRIGLIONE No. Thank you, no. (*He crosses to the exit*) I
haven't got the guts to play that kind of poker.
(*JUDGE CORRIGLIONE unbolts the door and leaves the room
without another word. We see him climbing up the stairs
to the ground level, his shoulders slumped. The players
look silently at the door. RAFFERTY crosses to the door and
passes the heavy bolt again, locking it. As MALEY deals,
LOOMIS picks up the legal document and weighs it in his
hand*)

LOOMIS What if the President asks our friend Mr. Bruce Bellingham to boil this down into three pungent paragraphs?

RAFFERTY Bellingham won't see it. Because you'll get it back
from Griff tonight. Signed.

WEBSTER Why does Griff keep Bellingham in the top drawer?

RAFFERTY He reads. He's a pair of glasses. Don't worry,
Charlie. Nobody in politics stands still. Any day now you'll
find Mr. Bellingham in the wastebasket.

MALEY There's them as is in, and them as is out.

RAFFERTY Axel, tell our friends what you found out about Mr.
Bruce Bellingham.

MALEY (*Beaming*) A big fat fascinating nothing.

DOC What good is that?

MALEY For eighteen months he was someplace; and *nobody*
—but nobody—knows where.

LOOMIS You think he was in prison?

RAFFERTY We'll find out.

WEBSTER Griff ought to know about this.

RAFFERTY When you draw an ace, Charlie, you don't stick it
in your hatband. (*Throwing in his cards*) I'm out. (RAFFERTY
gets up and walks over to the piano) We having any enter-
tainment for Griff tonight?

MALEY The La Reve Sisters are coming over.

DOC Who're *they?*

MALEY It's a dancing and singing act. They dance, mostly. I
got 'em from that club on K Street where they serve very old
ginger ale.
  (*Intermittently* RAFFERTY *pokes one finger at the piano,
  thinking.* WEBSTER *and* LOOMIS *compare hands.* LOOMIS
  takes in the pot)

WEBSTER What ever happened to that girl Griff used to see all
the time in New York, when he was a Senator?

MALEY Claire Jones?

LOOMIS She was a pretty one. Too bad he had to give her up.

DOC Bedfellows make strange politics.

MALEY How about something fancy this time? Spit in the
ocean? Or deuces, treys, and one-eyed queens wild? (*All
look at him dourly*) O.K., straight draw.
  (HASTINGS *appears at the top of the stairs and starts to de-
  scend. His hat brim is turned down over his face, and he*

has turned up the collar of his topcoat to help conceal his identity. HASTINGS *knocks. The players look at each other questioningly.* MALEY *springs to the door, and speaks through it, with his hand on the bolt)*

MALEY   Who is it?

HASTINGS   *(Through the door)* Mr. John Smith. *(They all know who "Mr. John Smith" is, and they spring up, pushing back their chairs as* MALEY *unlocks the door eagerly, and swings it open.* RAFFERTY *strikes a welcoming chord on the piano.* HASTINGS *enters, takes off his hat and tosses it across the room into the easy chair)* I'm home! *(*RAFFERTY *helps him off with his coat, and we get a good look at the* PRESIDENT. *This is not quite the same man we saw before. The hair is a touch whiter, the face creased with a few more lines of responsibility, but he seems to be riding now on nervous energy. The* GANG, *although still showing deference for his office, seem much more cozy with him than they were six months before. There is a warm interchange of greetings)*

MALEY   We're very glad you could come, Mr. Smith! Everything's ready, Mr. Smith.
   *(*HASTINGS *crosses to the green felt table, and touches it affectionately)*

HASTINGS   Out of the mausoleum and back to the green pastures! Hi ya, Doc, Josh, Charlie.
   (The PRESIDENT *chuckles, crosses to the upholstered chair)*

LOOMIS   We've been missing you, amigo.

HASTINGS   Do you know how many times I've wanted to come to these shindigs? But every fifteen minutes something comes up that makes it impossible for the country to stay in business! *(He sits.* DOC *has been fixing a stiff highball for*

the PRESIDENT; *now he crosses and hands it to him*) I'd better not. There's tomorrow morning.
(*He waves it away. But* DOC *insists*)

DOC This is a prescription. A gargle. But swallow it.
(HASTINGS *smiles, then shrugs*)

HASTINGS Doctor's orders!
(*They all drink with him*)

WEBSTER Now that Mr. Smith is here, we've crossed over to the good stuff.

MALEY I got this in New York from a very distinguished boot-legger.

HASTINGS While you fellas have been taking each other's money, I've been closeted for three-and-a-half hours with Arthur Anderson, the British Ambassador, and twenty State Department ginks who have sitting muscles made out of cast iron. I got Arthur Anderson in the men's room so he could tell me what it was all about, and he got me so confused I forgot to go to the toilet! (*They all laugh*) I suppose some place there's a book that gives you the facts on all this stuff. But who's got time to read a book? Hell, I shouldn't belly-ache about it. (*Getting up*) Let's play poker!
(*He gets up and takes his place at the table*)

RAFFERTY Charlie. Crack out a fresh pack for the head man.

WEBSTER (*Handing* HASTINGS *an unopened pack of cards*) Never been touched by human hands.

HASTINGS Why, thank you, Charlie. How've you been? Taking good care of the veterans?

WEBSTER Doing my best.

HASTINGS Taking good care of Charlie?

WEBSTER Haven't won a hand yet tonight.

HASTINGS Well, the sucker just got here and the evening's young! Who's the banker?

RAFFERTY What do you need?

HASTINGS Oh, five hundred for a starter.
  (MALEY *has "freshened" the* PRESIDENT's *drink with about four fingers of straight bourbon and placed the glass in front of him on the poker table. Anticipating the game,* HASTINGS *sips from it, not realizing it is a new drink*)

MALEY You ought to give 'em the slip more often, Prez.

HASTINGS (*As he deals*) It's a neat trick, shaking the Secret Service boys. With my hat brim turned down, and my coat collar turned up so nobody'll recognize me, every step of the way I feel like Mata Hari. (*He picks up his own hand and taps the cards emphatically on the table*) Why? A butcher goes home at night, he forgets all about hindquarters of beef. And the next morning he's a better butcher. My barber doesn't spend the whole night shaving people. If he did, I'd have one less ear! (*All have picked up their hands, arranged their cards, and are studying them*) Are we playing jacks or better? Who's got 'em?
  (*All pass until we come to* RAFFERTY)

RAFFERTY (*Clears his throat*) I'll open.
  (*He pushes in some chips. Everybody stays*)

HASTINGS Let's make this a respectable pot, boys. (*Putting in a stack*) This is the first chance I've had to raise the Attorney General. (*Looks around the table at the others, who are taking their cue from* RAFFERTY. *The* PRESIDENT *feigns a*

Southern accent) Now don't let mah little-ole blue chips get lonely!

(*Everybody stays except* LOOMIS, *who moistens his lips, so that we sense he has four aces. He tosses in his cards*)

LOOMIS I'm out.

HASTINGS Tough, Josh. Better luck next time around.

LOOMIS Sure.

RAFFERTY I'll stay.

HASTINGS Cards? (*He hands out draws*) What the hell is there about a piece of pasteboard that *feels* so good in your fingers? (*With euphoria from every pore*) You get around a table with people you like, and once in a while you get a hand you like, and it's almost something physical—like holding five beautiful women.

MALEY Kee-ripes! He's got five queens! I'm getting out of here.

HASTINGS (*Beaming at his hand*) I'll play along with these. (*Reactions from all the players: the* PRESIDENT *has a good hand*)

RAFFERTY (*Tossing in some chips*) Into the pat hand.

HASTINGS Bunch of hot shots here. O.K., sports. (*He raises considerably. He loves the quiet tension which hovers in the air around the table.* WEBSTER *throws in his cards, glances at* RAFFERTY *with an expression which says, "I just threw away one helluva hand"*) Water too deep for you, Charlie?

MALEY (*Throwing in his cards*) I can't bluff this gang with a pair of sixes.

(*He gets up and goes for the cigars*)

DOC (*Matching the bet*) I can still swim.

RAFFERTY (*Pushing in his chips*) Call.

HASTINGS (*Showing his cards*) Ten high straight.
(DOC *has a flush, but* RAFFERTY'S *eyes tell him to throw it in. He does*)

RAFFERTY (*Showing his cards*) Couple of more kings out of work.
(HASTINGS *chortles happily and pulls in the pot*)

HASTINGS Why can't I get this lucky in the market? Where'd you dig up those tips you gave me, Ax? You got a broker in the Kremlin?

RAFFERTY (*Innocently*) Yeah, Ax. We all got stung.

MALEY I was a bull when I should have been a bear. (*He places cigars on the table*) Gentlemen, compliments of yesterday's Cuban Government.
(*They all light their cigars*)

HASTINGS During the campaign, I had the cockeyed idea that Cabinet meetings could be like this: a box of cigars in the middle of the table; we'd read over the mail together; then we'd deal out who-does-what, have a drink or two, and call it a day. No such luck. Your deal, Charlie.
(HASTINGS *is now on his third highball, but apparently doesn't realize it, nor does he show any signs of intoxication.* HASTINGS *cuts,* WEBSTER *deals, and everybody antes in*)

LOOMIS (*Taking the cards, clears his throat.*) Why don't we have a Cabinet meeting right now, for about fifteen seconds?

RAFFERTY Hell, don't bother Griff with any business tonight. Unless it's damned important.

(LOOMIS *reaches back into the pocket of his coat, which is draped over the chair behind him*)

LOOMIS You know I wouldn't do that, amigo. (*Fumbling*) We've got a little foul-up over at Interior—you know, one of those blamed duplications, with everybody steppin' on everybody else's toes. (*Shrugs*) There's just one way to clear up the whole thing. A little old executive order.

(*He tosses the blue-backed legal document to* HASTINGS, *who scowls at it*)

HASTINGS Don't make me read anything.

LOOMIS Well, I've been over it pretty careful. (HASTINGS *is browsing gloomily through the paper.* LOOMIS *affects a sudden change of heart, and tries to take back the document.* DOC, *embarrassed, rises quickly and crosses to the bar for a drink.* MALEY *is pouring drinks at the table*) I'm an ornery bastard, pestering you on your night out. Forget about it.

(MALEY *crosses to the bar.* RAFFERTY *stops the nervous* LOOMIS *from grabbing the paper*)

RAFFERTY I've read it. It's all right. Corriglione went over it, too.

HASTINGS Oh? What did the Judge say?

RAFFERTY It's legal. Read it if you want to. We'll wait for you.

(RAFFERTY *uncaps pen and holds it for* HASTINGS. HASTINGS *laughs a little at this, then riffles to the last page and prepares to write his name. But something in the document seems to catch his eye, and he turns back to the preceding page. Each watcher holds his breath. The* PRESIDENT *seems uneasy. He knows he shouldn't be signing a "blank check" in this cursory fashion. But he sees the poker hand, face down on the table. Then he looks across the table thoughtfully at* LOOMIS)

HASTINGS   Josh. If you were President, and I asked you to sign this, would you do it?

(*A moment's pause*)

LOOMIS   I scarcely think I'd be inclined to question an old friend's judgment.

(*A breath more of hesitation. Then* HASTINGS *quickly scrawls his name, and grins as he passes the paper back to the relieved* LOOMIS. MALEY *returns to his seat at the table*)

HASTINGS   At least this Administration accomplished something today.

RAFFERTY   I thought for a minute you were going to call in Cavendish for a consultation.

(*There is the nervous laughter of relieved tension*)

WEBSTER   I wonder if old Stone Face can play poker.

(DOC *wanders back to his seat*)

LOOMIS   Don't ask me to teach him.

MALEY   Whenever I play with millionaires, they always set a ten-cent limit.

HASTINGS   That's why they're millionaires.

(*They all laugh.* HASTINGS *and the rest of the* GANG *are examining their cards.* HIGGY *appears at the top of the outside staircase, and seems even fatter as he waddles carefully down the narrow stairs. He knocks at the door.* MALEY *and* RAFFERTY *exchange glances*)

MALEY   The girls wasn't supposed to be here until one o'clock.

HASTINGS   Girls?

(MALEY *crosses to the door*)

MALEY   (*His hand on the bolt, speaking through the door*) Laverne, honey? (HIGGY *doesn't answer*) Renee?

(*Again, a pause.* MALEY *looks baffled.* HASTINGS, *who has been looking at his cards, suddenly pushes back his chair and rises*)

HASTINGS   Hell, it's that cable from Downing Street.

RAFFERTY   Who knows you're here?

HASTINGS   Only Bruce. Let him in.
(*As the door swings open, the bulbous* HIGGY *enters*)

HIGGY (*Puts his hat on the bar*)   Gentlemen. Good evening, Mr. President. (HASTINGS *is puzzled, but he assumes* HIGGINS *has been invited. The players look at the New Jersey politician as if he were Friday roast beef at a convent. Safely in the door, he looks around the room with malign good humor*) How ya been? (*Turning to* HASTINGS) You remember me, Mr. President?

HASTINGS   Of course—New Jersey.

RAFFERTY   What are you doing out of Camden, Higgy?

HIGGY   I sent you a change-of-address card, Mr. Rafferty; maybe the Postmaster General isn't up to the level of the rest of the Cabinet.

HASTINGS   If you've come to play poker, play poker.
(HIGGY *floats*)

HIGGY   I'll just watch. (*Smoothly*) It would represent a change of policy for this Administration to deal me in.
(RAFFERTY *gives* HIGGY *a disintegrating look.* HIGGY *doesn't disintegrate. A little uncomfortably, the game proceeds; but* HIGGY, *over their shoulders, glancing at several of the hands, is a source of irritation. The following conversation lies against a counterpoint of desultory betting.* DOC *opens.*

All stay. WEBSTER *deals the cards.* MALEY *clutches his cards to his chest as* HIGGY *peers over his shoulder*)

DOC (*Staring straight at* HIGGY's *belt buckle*) Rumor is rampant, Higgy, that you will not even be entered this year in the Atlantic City beauty contest.

HIGGY I've left New Jersey. (*He crosses upstage for a cigar*) Y'see, I caught a little chill at the convention. And when I got home, even Asbury Park began to feel like Alaska.

MALEY There's them as is in, and them as is out. (*Tossing in his cards*) I'm out.

HIGGY Oh, I'm not "out." I'm a District of Columbia citizen now. Nice place, isn't it? Although the summers *do* get warm. (*Studying* WEBSTER's *cards thoughtfully, as* WEBSTER *bets*) Now I wonder, Charles, if your hand is as strong as you think it is.

HASTINGS Mr. Higgins, poker is the order of business; if you're not going to play, what can we do for you?

HIGGY I was thinking maybe I could do something for you, sir, and for the boys here.

RAFFERTY Such as?

HIGGY In my new job as investigator for the Hearn Committee I'm being asked to do something that just pains me. Anybody got a light? (WEBSTER *passes a lighter to* HIGGY *without enthusiasm*) Thanks, Charles. (*Kindling his cigar*) I wonder if you realize how interested Senator Hearn is in everything you gentlemen are doing.
(*The* GANG *is very still*)

HASTINGS What about Senator Hearn?

HIGGY Well, his subcommittee might bump into some very colorful information; and then again, it might not. (*Admiring the lighter as he gives it back to* WEBSTER) Hmmm, eighteen carats! Was this a gift from a grateful veteran?

HASTINGS (*Irked*) Mr. Higgins, we came here to play poker.

HIGGY So did I. (*With piety*) And all of us being dedicated to good, clean, honest government—

RAFFERTY Griff, the Reverend Higgins is the gentleman who once offered to sell Jersey City to Manhattan for fifteen cents.

HASTINGS What's he selling now?

HIGGY Not a thing, Mr. President. I've just got a taxpayer's healthy curiosity about certain administrative departments. The Veterans' Bureau, for example.

WEBSTER (*Rising irritably*) Anything you want to know about the Veterans' Bureau, just come to me. My files are open at any time to any authorized agency, including the Hearn Committee.

(HIGGY's *facile air changes into one of deadly authority*)

HIGGY Quit bluffing. I've seen your hand.

HASTINGS (*Rising, indignantly to* HIGGY) Get the hell out of here.

HIGGY Mr. President. I thought I was doing the Administration a service by coming to you before I reported to Senator Hearn.

HASTINGS If you mean to imply any reflection on my friends, I won't even dignify your insolence by asking for an apology!
(HIGGY *moves toward the door*)

HIGGY O.K. O.K., sir. I came here because I feel sorry for these poor sons-of-bitches you call your friends. They're gonna get hung higher than the Washington Monument.

RAFFERTY Go home, Higgy. Your mother's barking for you.

MALEY (*A little nervously*) Walt, maybe we shouldn't oughta—

RAFFERTY Go home, Higgy!
(RAFFERTY *holds the door open.* HIGGY *resumes his insolent pleasantry*)

HIGGY You've got my phone number, Walter.
(HIGGY *lumbers up the stairs.* RAFFERTY *slams and bolts the door. There is a pause.* HASTINGS *has held his cards, waiting for the game to get started again. Now he throws down the hand violently, and the cards splatter*)

HASTINGS (*Crosses to the bar to get a drink*) Damn it all! Where can I go? (*He pours himself a strong slug, which he downs; then he starts to prepare another*) I try to get away from the yapping and the yelling and Frances trying to sweat me into a suit of silver armor. I want to play cards with my friends! (*He crosses to the armchair and sits*) And this cockroach comes crawling out of the woodwork.
(*He kills off half the drink in his hand*)

MALEY (*Pointing to the chips*) You're lucky tonight, Prez. Don't quit while you're winning.

RAFFERTY Who could have told Higgins you were here?

HASTINGS Nobody knows. I didn't tell anybody, except Bruce. He doesn't even know Higgins.

RAFFERTY Doesn't he?

(*The* PRESIDENT *is feeling his drinks now.* BELLINGHAM *hurries down the outside stairs*)

MALEY Play cards, Prez. Don't think about anything. Not tonight. Play cards. (HASTINGS *doesn't react.* MALEY *speaks with forced brightness*) Say, did you hear the one about the Siamese twins on their honeymoon? And one of 'em turned to the other one and said—

(BELLINGHAM *knocks at the door. Nobody moves. The knock is repeated.* MALEY *dances to the door*)

MALEY Girls?

BELLINGHAM (*Through the door*) It's Bellingham.

MALEY Aw, nuts! (MALEY *looks back into the room for instructions. The poker players are mute*)

HASTINGS Let him in.

(MALEY *passes the bolt and opens the door.* BELLINGHAM *enters and crosses directly to the* PRESIDENT. *He takes an envelope from his pocket and offers it to* HASTINGS, *who stares at it*)

BELLINGHAM I brought this directly from the decoding room, Mr. President. It's from Downing Street. The Prime Minister still has a number of questions.

HASTINGS The Prime Minister will have to wait until tomorrow.

BELLINGHAM It's already "tomorrow" in London.

HASTINGS Well, London can go on our time for a change. Tell 'em that, and tell me something. Did you ever meet a fat boy from New Jersey, named Higgins?

BELLINGHAM Yes, sir.

HASTINGS Did you tell him I was here tonight?
(*There is a brief pause*)

BELLINGHAM I got the impression Mr. Higgins was an old
friend, someone who knew all of you intimately.

LOOMIS I know my dentist intimately. But I don't want to
have my teeth drilled at a poker party.

BELLINGHAM All right. I told Higgins.

HASTINGS When I tell you I'm going some place, I don't want
to read about it in the *New York Times* before I get there.

BELLINGHAM Mr. President, Higgins has been after me, for
weeks. I didn't pay any attention to him, until he began
hinting at some pretty damaging things. Not about you, sir,
but about some of the people in this room. (WEBSTER *gets to
his feet, indignantly*) If he's lying, somebody'd better shut
him up. If he's telling the truth—
(HASTINGS *rises and crosses to the side table slowly. He
takes a fresh bottle of bourbon and empties some of it
into his glass. He then pours a drink for* BELLINGHAM)

HASTINGS Ax. Right now would be a very good time for you
to make a joke.

RAFFERTY Griff, if you believe the blathering of that paranoiac
fat boy, you better get yourself another Attorney General.

HASTINGS (*Downing the drink*) Sit down, Walt.

RAFFERTY Put Mr. Bellingham in! He seems so hot on justice.
We came down to Washington because you said you *had*
to have us. You dragged us out of some pretty high-paying
private practices. I don't know what Mr. Interim was dragged

away from. And some of us are pretty curious, by the way.
(HASTINGS *crosses directly to* BELLINGHAM)

HASTINGS Bruce, how many drinks have you had this evening?

BELLINGHAM None.

HASTINGS You've got some catching up to do. (*He hands the glass to* BELLINGHAM, *who merely holds it*) Haven't you heard about "All Work and No Play"? Drink it! What do you want to be a troublemaker for? We're gonna play poker together. Whose deal is it? Give Bruce a hand! You're all gonna like him as soon as you start taking his money! (*The* PRESIDENT *starts to pick up his splattered cards. As he bends over to get some that have fallen to the floor, he seems to teeter on the brink of nausea*) I don't feel exactly great, Doc. You got something in your little black bag you can give me?

DOC I'm not sure—

HASTINGS (*Grabbing* DOC *by the shoulder roughly and spinning him around*) "You're not sure"! What the hell kind of a doctor are you, Doc? You oughta see the stack of letters I've got on my desk from the A.M.A.! Every damned M.D. in the country is yelling bloody murder because the President's personal physician is a chiropractor! (*Softening quickly, clapping* DOC *sentimentally on the shoulder like an old comrade at arms*) I'll stick by ya. Don't you worry, Doc. I'll stick by ya. I'll stick by ya.

(*During the above,* LAVERNE, RENEE, *and the* PIANO PLAYER *come down the steps*)

LOOMIS Come on, amigo. We've got a nice deck of Bicycles all warmed up.

(LAVERNE *knocks: three raps, then two*)

MALEY   Here comes some medicine for ya, Prez. (*He scurries to the door*) Laverne? Renee? (*The girls giggle.* HASTINGS *sinks into his chair at the poker table.* MALEY *opens the door and ushers in the* LA REVE SISTERS *and the* PIANO PLAYER. *The girls are jazzy flappers, beaded and bespangled.* LAVERNE *has a very sincere bustline and she's a talker.* RENEE *is a shapely pair of legs surmounted by a sloe-eyed, vacuous face*) Fellas, these are the La Reve Sisters.

LAVERNE   I'm Laverne.

RENEE   And I'm Renee.

LAVERNE   La Reve means "The Dream." It's French.

DOC   Piano player, let's have some music.
   (PIANO PLAYER *crosses to the piano*)

RAFFERTY   Let's turn off some of these lights.
   (WEBSTER *switches off the main lights*)

MALEY   (*Leading* LAVERNE *by the arm toward* HASTINGS)
   Girls, I want you to meet Mr. Smith. He's the guest of honor.
   (The girls, *who know exactly what is expected of them, push out a coy greeting*)

LAVERNE   Pleased to meetcha, Smitty.

RENEE   Ooooo, he's cute.

LAVERNE   Say! Did anybody ever tell you that you look almost exactly like—
   (PIANO PLAYER *starts to play*)

RAFFERTY   Yeah. Everybody tells him. Don't they, Smitty?

RENEE   He *does* look exactly like—

MALEY (*Puts his arm aroud* RENEE *and pulls her aside*) Shut up, honey. (*Aloud*) Ain't they knockouts? Renee ain't got much upstairs—but what a staircase!

LAVERNE (*To* HASTINGS) You want to dance, big boy?
(HASTINGS' *eyes are on* BELLINGHAM, *sensing his disapproval*)

HASTINGS Sure, sure! Why not?

LAVERNE Say, you are cute.
(HASTINGS *begins to dance awkwardly, still looking at* BELLINGHAM)

LAVERNE (*Over* HASTINGS' *shoulder, pointing to* DOC) Renee, why don't you dance with that one? (*To* HASTINGS) Renee's always had a "pash" for soldier boys.
(RENEE *starts to dance with* DOC)

LAVERNE (*Chattering to* HASTINGS *as they dance*) We call ourselves the La Reve Sisters, but we're not actually sisters. My first partner was my cousin. She was lousy. In this business, it's not blood that counts, it's talent.
(BELLINGHAM *crosses to the door, chagrined by this demonstration.* HASTINGS *sees him leaving*)

HASTINGS (*Shouting*) Hey! Hey, you! (*The* PRESIDENT's *raised voice stops* BELLINGHAM) Where do you think you're going, Mr. Bellingham? Don't you like the company? (BELLINGHAM *looks away. The* PRESIDENT *bellows at him furiously*) Look at me! (*The* PIANO PLAYER *stops playing. All other activity in the room freezes*) What's the matter? You want me to act as if I'd already been stamped on a fifty-dollar bill?

LAVERNE Just try to have a good time, honey.

HASTINGS (*Pulling her up onto the poker table, using a chair as a step*) I'll show you how to have a good time! (*He shouts*) Music!! Loud music! (*Atop the poker table,* HASTINGS *and* LAVERNE *start to dance with violent energy.* BELLINGHAM *watches, staring up at* HASTINGS *with a wondering dismay and pity.* HASTINGS *stops dancing and thunders down at him over the honky-tonk music*) Stop looking at me like that. You hear me? I don't want you around. I don't want you around the White House! I don't want you around my life! Get out! Get out! (BELLINGHAM *leaves.* HASTINGS *jumps down from the table and rushes out of the door after him, still shouting.* DOC *and* WEBSTER *restrain the* PRESIDENT *from running up the stairs into the street. As* HASTINGS *wheels back into the room, he looks around the circle of his friends. He is sickened by the growing suspicion that these men are destroying him. Hoarsely, he throws the last words at* WEBSTER) Get out!

(WEBSTER *turns away.* HASTINGS *is a lost and bewildered figure as the lights fade*)

The Curtain Falls

(*In the darkness, we hear the buzz of the White House switchboard. A glow comes onto the curtain, then over the loudspeakers we hear a White House operator. The calls are punctuated by the buzzes and clicks of the incoming calls*)

OPERATOR'S VOICE White House. One moment. I'll connect you with the Security Chief.

White House. Mr. Bellingham is no longer here. He can be reached at the Senate Office Building.

White House. The Press Secretary is busy. Will you hold the line, please?

White House. I'm sorry, Senator. No calls are being put through to the President's office. All his appointments have been canceled for the day. Thank you, sir.

I can give you the Press Secretary now. Thank you for waiting.

White House. Yes, Long Distance? We've been unable to reach the President. Will you ask Mexico City to try Secretary Anderson at the State Department? National 2-100.

White House. Mrs. Hastings is out of the city for the Christmas holidays. She's expected back tomorrow. I'll give you the Appointment Secretary.

White House. One moment. I'll connect you.

White House. I'm sorry, Mr. Maley. The President still hasn't returned. I'll leave word how many times you've called. As soon as he comes in.

(*The voice and the buzzes begin to fade as soon as the change in scenery has been completed*)

White House. That line is busy. Will you wait?

White House. I'll connect you with the Chief Steward.

White House. We are unable to reach the President. I'll report that you called, Mr. Secretary.

I'm sorry. There's no answer in the Chief Steward's office.

White House. One moment, please. I'll connect you.

(*The sound fades away as the lights come up on the following scene*)

SCENE 2

Scene: The sitting room of the Presidential apartment in the White House. It is early in January of the following year. The gloom of twilight makes the room seem more tired and cheerless than before. A Christmas tree rises in the corner and some impersonal Christmas decorations are hung around the room. FRANCES *enters, wearing furs, and carrying an ample handbag, which she treats protectively.* COBB *follows her in, carrying a traveling case.* FRANCES *goes behind the desk, and pulls off her gloves with hurried impatience, as if there is a great deal for her to do. She calls toward the inner rooms.*

FRANCES Griffith?

COBB The President isn't here, Mrs. Hastings.

FRANCES Where is he?

COBB I don't know, Madam. He left at seven-fifteen this morning. Alone. Except for the driver and the Secret Service people.

FRANCES Where did he go?

COBB The staff was not informed. He didn't expect you back until tomorrow.

FRANCES (*Going to the phone*) Central, get Walter Rafferty for me. (*To* COBB) These decorations should be removed. The holiday season is over.

89

COBB   Yes, Mrs. Hastings.

FRANCES   As I came in, I noticed Mr. Bellingham downstairs.

COBB   He's been waiting all afternoon to see the President.

FRANCES   The President left instructions that he doesn't want to see Mr. Bellingham.

COBB   He was told that.

FRANCES   (*Into phone*) Hello. Walter? Just a moment. (*Covering the mouthpiece*) Mr. Cobb, tell Mr. Bellingham that in the President's absence I will see him (COBB *nods and goes out.* FRANCES *continues to talk into phone*) Walter, I came back from Wilmont a day early. I have to see you immediately. It concerns your friend, Axel Maley. (*She draws some deposit slips out of her purse*) While I was home, one of the officers of the Gibraltar Bank gave me some rather startling information. I can't tell you on the phone, Walter. It's something I've got to show you in person. (*Pause*) No, I haven't told Griffith. Where is he, do you know? (*Knock*) Just a moment. (*Calling*) Will you wait, please? (*Into phone*) Not here, not at the White House. All right, I'll meet you there as quickly as I can. (*She hangs up, then quickly puts the deposit slips back into her purse*) Come in.

  (BELLINGHAM *enters*)

BELLINGHAM   Thank you for seeing me, Mrs. Hastings.

FRANCES   I'm afraid you're wasting your time. The President just won't see you.

BELLINGHAM   Then may I talk to you for a few minutes?

FRANCES   Why?

BELLINGHAM   I need your help.

FRANCES In connection with your work for the Hearn Committee?

BELLINGHAM I think Senator Hearn would fire me if he knew why I'm here.

FRANCES (*Rising*) Bruce, I don't know the reason the President discharged you, but I do know you've hurt him very deeply by going to work for a man who's trying to smear him.

BELLINGHAM That's not what he wants to do, Mrs. Hastings. But he's accumulated some pretty terrifying facts about men close to the President. The President's got to know about them.

FRANCES Is that why you're here?

BELLINGHAM Somebody's got to tell him.

FRANCES Does it occur to you that other people are looking after the President's welfare?

BELLINGHAM Then please persuade him to listen to me.

FRANCES I'll try. But later. Not today. I'll call you at your office. (*Picking up her purse*) Now, if you'll excuse me, I have an appointment outside the White House.
    (*Resignedly* BRUCE *crosses with* FRANCES *toward the door, but* HASTINGS *enters. He seems preoccupied, depressed*)

HASTINGS (*To Bellingham, with a quiet bitterness*) Get out.

BELLINGHAM Mr. President—

HASTINGS Just get out.

FRANCES Bruce is my guest. He came here to see me.

91

HASTINGS (*Turns to* FRANCES) What are you doing back from Wilmont, Duchess? Couldn't you take the Greeleys, even with Christmas ribbons?

FRANCES Where have you been all day, Griffith?

HASTINGS Out at Bethesda. (*He puts his hat and coat on chair, then draws a bottle of medicine from his pocket. It is ink-like and remarkably similar to his predecessor's*) If those doctors had any brains, they'd know this stuff isn't going to do any good. (*Puts bottle on the desk*)

FRANCES You're not sick?

HASTINGS President juice. That's all this is. The doctors are very disappointed in me. I'm all right. But don't let it out that I've been at the Navy Hospital all day. (*He sits on the couch*) The stock market'll go down eleven points. And we can't afford it.

FRANCES You musn't be sick, Griffith. Don't even joke about it. (*The phone rings.* FRANCES *picks it up*) Hello? No, no. You've got to wait for me, Walter. I'm coming right now. (*She hangs up*)

HASTINGS What does Walt want?

FRANCES We can talk about it later. (*She starts to go*) Griffith, I think you should listen to Mr. Bellingham.

BELLINGHAM Mr. President—

HASTINGS I don't want to hear any more from you. Come back in a few years, Mr. Interim. You can help shoe in a new President.

BELLINGHAM Give me five minutes. Then throw me out if you want to.

FRANCES Please, Griffith.

HASTINGS O.K. Five minutes.

(HASTINGS *takes out his watch and puts it on the desk*)

FRANCES (*Crossing*) I'll be back almost immediately.

(BELLINGHAM *waits for* FRANCES *to leave and then addresses* HASTINGS *with businesslike intensity*)

BELLINGHAM Mr. President, may I speak to you as if you were still an editor and I'm bringing you a news story?

HASTINGS Go ahead.

BELLINGHAM The day after I left my desk here, Senator Hearn offered me a job with his committee. I turned him down, because I knew all he wanted was to pick my brains. But after I started hearing things around Washington, I changed my mind. I took the job because I thought I could help you.

HASTINGS How?

BELLINGHAM Higgins wasn't bluffing. He *knows!*

HASTINGS Knows what? *What* does he know!?

BELLINGHAM My God, Mr. President, don't *you* know?

HASTINGS (*Rising*) You want to talk to me like a newspaperman? O.K.! But there's one thing I insist on as an editor. I want to know the *reliability* of the source. I wouldn't believe Higgy if he told me January first was New Year's Day!

BELLINGHAM Then believe me.

HASTINGS Who are you? For eighteen months, nobody knew where you were. Walt says you were in jail. Is that true? Do you want to tell me what you were doing?

BELLINGHAM I'll tell you what I wasn't doing, Mr. President. I wasn't stealing a million dollars a month from the Veterans' Bureau. I didn't have my fingers up to the shoulders in bootleg graft, like your Department of so-called Justice!

HASTINGS Answer my question.

BELLINGHAM All right. I'll tell you what I was doing, and I'm ashamed of it, because I was running away. (*He speaks quietly, his face turned away from the* PRESIDENT) I joined an order.

HASTINGS What?

BELLINGHAM I was a novice, in a place way off in the mountains, where you give up your life; you even give up your name. I was "Brother Pacificus." I went there because I thought they could teach me some kind of faith. But faith isn't something you can learn; it's something that happens to you. (BELLINGHAM's *tone becomes bitterly back-to-earth*) Back in Washington, at least I've been part of the human race. Not a very proud part. I think I'd rather be a jackal, or a self-respecting typhoid germ.

HASTINGS (*Crossing to him*) Idealism was last year. They voted it out.

BELLINGHAM It's not idealism to recognize a fact.

HASTINGS (*Sitting on the sofa*) Give me a fact.

BELLINGHAM All right. (*Graphically, gesturing around the room*) This is the Veterans' Hospital outside Louisville, Kentucky, a site chosen by the Honorable Charles Webster because of its proximity to that great American institution, the Kentucky Derby. (*Drawing a door in the air with his forefingers*) Through this door come in the bed sheets and blankets and bandages for the somewhat bent tin soldiers who didn't duck quite quickly enough. Let's just look at the bed sheets. Here they come, clean and cool and fresh, and God, how they're needed! But Mr. Webster's inspector— carefully schooled in what he's expected to do—opens up a package of two hundred, looks at the top sheet— (BELL- INGHAM *pantomimes examining a sheet, finding something wrong with it*) "Oh! Oh! This sheet is torn! Can't allow our boys to sleep on defective merchandise! Condemn the whole carload!" Mind you, that sheet really *was* torn, the *top* sheet! But the other hundred and ninety-nine in every batch were the best bed sheets money could buy, and the government paid for them, two dollars and ten cents apiece. But thirty cents a sheet is the *most* you can expect to get for "Condemned Merchandise." And who just *happens* to buy them up at a fraction of cost? The original manufacturer! (*With an expansive gesture of mockery*) He's delighted! He can shut off his power, lay off his help, and keep sending the same carload back to the same Veterans' Hospital so that the same inspector can mark down the same bed sheets and keep carting them back to him. Perpetual motion! And every time around, the government pays the full price for every sheet!—while the aching bastards in the wards sleep on bare mattresses and bed springs. Naturally, this manu- facturer is making enough profit to afford a few Christmas presents. And in Mr. Webster's office, it's Christmas almost every week!

HASTINGS I don't believe it.

BELLINGHAM Senator Hearn does. Because he has a locked file containing invoices, bills of lading, swatches from marked sheets that the government has bought as many as twenty-five times, and sworn affidavits from three inspectors who got scared.

(HASTINGS *is immobile. After a pause, he seizes the telephone*)

HASTINGS Find Walter Rafferty for me. (*He slams down the phone*) If this is so damned well documented, why hasn't that headline-crazy Senator issued some subpoenas?

BELLINGHAM There's one piece missing. He's trying to trace down where the money goes. Do you suppose Mr. Rafferty can supply any information on this subject?

HASTINGS As an investigator, you mean?

BELLINGHAM No, sir, that is *not* what I mean.

HASTINGS Damn it, Walt is my best friend. I appointed him to hunt down exactly this kind of immorality in government.

BELLINGHAM I only want to say that Mr. Rafferty has not been spending his time in a monastery.
(*He sits*)

HASTINGS (*Pacing*) In anything as big, as new, as the Veterans' Administration, people make mistakes. Honest mistakes. We'll get them cleaned up. Walt will.

BELLINGHAM Mr. President. Do you know about the "honest mistake" called "the fish bowl"?

HASTINGS What does that mean?

BELLINGHAM Once a week some joker from the Justice Department makes a business trip to Manhattan. He takes a hotel room, different hotel every week. Correction: he takes *two* hotel rooms, adjoining. On a table in the center of one room he puts a fish bowl. The door to the hallway is unlocked, and the fisherman sits in the next room with his eye at the keyhole. At fifteen minute intervals, assorted gentlemen drop by, each depositing a thousand fish into the bowl. The eye behind the keyhole checks off the names on a list, and makes sure none of the fingers are sticky. Curiously enough, Senator Hearn has a man on the same floor with a lovely view of the elevator; not only is he making a list, he's taking pictures. To the surprise of nobody, this Photo Album turns out to be the "Who's Who" of the Alcoholic Beverage Profession. Can you guess how many of these fish bowl regulars have been indicted by your Justice Department? Not one!

HASTINGS If Senator Hearn has a list of lawbreakers, why doesn't he do something about it? He doesn't have to wade through an indictment, he can call a cop on the corner.

BELLINGHAM He doesn't care about a few bootleggers or the character who checks off the list; he wants to know where the money's going. There seems to be a welfare fund for building a playground and rest home for retired Army and Navy officers at Key West, but there isn't any such place at Key West.

HASTINGS Does Pacificus mean "Peaceful"?

BELLINGHAM That's right, sir.

HASTINGS How the hell did you ever get a name like that? (*Abruptly,* FRANCES *hurries into the room. She is nervous and excited.* RAFFERTY *is at her heels, and he, too, seems disturbed and indignant*)

RAFFERTY Frances is all steamed up, Griff, and obviously there's something here that we'll have to look into.

97

HASTINGS (*Crossing to* RAFFERTY) I've been trying to get you, Walt. We've got some housecleaning to do.

RAFFERTY I've trusted Ax the same as you have!

HASTINGS What's this got to do with Ax?

FRANCES (*Behind the desk, pulling the deposit slips out of her purse*) Look at these, Griffith.

RAFFERTY Just a minute, Frances. Let's not discuss this in front of Senator Hearn's messenger boy.
(*He nods toward* BELLINGHAM)

HASTINGS We're going to do a lot of discussing in front of him. You might as well get used to it.
(*He takes the deposit slips*)

FRANCES Mr. Maley has on deposit at the Gibraltar Trust in Wilmont more than one million, six hundred thousand dollars.
(HASTINGS *glances quickly at* BELLINGHAM. *His eyes widen. Is this the missing piece of the puzzle?*)

HASTINGS Holy God!

FRANCES How can a man making eight thousand dollars a year accumulate—

HASTINGS We've got to sit Ax down right away, and have him tell us where all this came from!
(*He indicates the deposit slips*)

RAFFERTY I just found out about it twenty minutes ago from Frances. It's just as much a shock to me as it is to you.

FRANCES We tried to get Mr. Maley on the telephone, but there wasn't any answer.

HASTINGS I want Ax here, in this room, with a complete explanation. Not tomorrow. Not Monday. Now! Bruce, find him. Get him over here.

(BELLINGHAM *starts toward the door*)

RAFFERTY (*Crosses to phone*) All right, if you're in such a big rush, I'll put some of the boys from the Department on it.

BELLINGHAM I'll find him.

(*He goes off*)

HASTINGS (*Calling after* BELLINGHAM) The Weldon Park. Look downstairs in the billiard room.

FRANCES Has Mr. Maley said anything to you, Walter, about speculations?

RAFFERTY I guess Ax has been doing pretty well in the market.

HASTINGS Not if he takes his own tips.

RAFFERTY Chances are the money isn't even his. Ax is a pretty public-spirited gent. I know he's treasurer or trustee for some welfare fund or other.

HASTINGS *What* fund?

RAFFERTY (*Goes to desk humidor for cigar*) Oh, that thing for retired Army-Navy officers at Key West.

HASTINGS (*With a sinking feeling*) God, not Ax! Not poor, funny little Ax ... !

RAFFERTY Stop worrying about it. We'll get Ax straightened around.

HASTINGS I want a complete list of his business transactions. What stocks was Ax in?

RAFFERTY   Some oils. And we all had a nice little gain on one new issue—(*He clips his cigar*) Universal Hospital Supply. Were you in on that, Griff?

HASTINGS   I hope to hell not. Were you?

RAFFERTY   I may have been.

HASTINGS   Charlie Webster's your boy, Walt. You wanted him in the Veterans' Bureau. And if there's any stink over there, *you* can help explain it.

RAFFERTY   You've been listening to that jailbird again.

HASTINGS   *What* jailbird?

RAFFERTY   That Bellingham.

HASTINGS   If that's a sample of the accuracy of your information, you're in trouble, Walt. You and Charlie Webster and I had better get this settled, before the newspapers settle it for us.

RAFFERTY   (*Crossing to table for a drink*)   Oh, Charlie's off on vacation. Didn't anybody tell you?

HASTINGS   Get him back.

RAFFERTY   I don't know if we can. He's on a boat.

HASTINGS   *What* boat?

RAFFERTY   How should I know *what* boat? Charlie's been working pretty hard. He needed a little rest.

HASTINGS   Where was he going? Bermuda? The Bahamas? Cuba?

RAFFERTY   Greece, I think.

HASTINGS (*Outraged*) Greece! He could see a few ruins right in his own office.

RAFFERTY (*He crosses downstage and offers a drink to* HASTINGS) Look, Griff, this is the same as any other business. We all have to blink once in a while at a padded expense account, or if somebody sticks an office stamp on a letter to his girl. Here.

(HASTINGS *ignores the drink* RAFFERTY *has poured for him*)

HASTINGS (*Brandishing the deposit slips*) This is one helluva lot of two-cent stamps.

RAFFERTY What are you, Griff, an old lady or a practical politician? (*He downs the drink and sits. His manner is easy and persuasive*) Why do you think I got into politics? I like it. I like the game. So do you. It's better than poker. And the green felt runs all the way from the White House lawn to the valleys of California. When the table's as big as that, you don't play penny ante.

FRANCES It's not a game. You're a public servant.

RAFFERTY Swell. I'll serve the people. And I'll do it the way it's always been done, the way the people, if they're honest, *expect* it to be done. (*Holding up a cigar*) A cigar manufacturer is also serving the public. And if he's smart, he can turn an awful lot of tobacco leaves into thousand-dollar bills. Bravo! More power to him.

HASTINGS There's a moral consideration—

RAFFERTY (*Rising*) In *politics?* Who are you—some dime-in-the-platter backstreet preacher? Don't give me that "morality" noise. That's for the hicks, the holy old ladies, and the softies buying cemetery plots at a thousand per cent markup.

You think this country was built on the Twenty-third Psalm? Hell, it came out of nerve and salesmanship and gut-tearing competition. How do you think old Cavendish got his eight hundred million? In a Sunday School?

HASTINGS I happen to know that Sam Cavendish is a deeply religious man.

RAFFERTY He can afford morality. He's rich enough. I'm not. Neither are you. The "land of plenty" for everybody except the politician, who sticks his head through the hole in the canvas and lets the goddamned free press sling mud balls at him. He can't run his business like a business, because it's never *his* business. It belongs to the blessed American public that doesn't give a hoot in hell until some poor bastard gets his pinky caught in the cash register! Name me a job that demands more and pays less than serving the American taxpayer. The Customers' Man can screw 'em blind on the Big Board. That's O.K. The Oil Boys can simmer the fat out of the ground, the Real Estate Sharps can bank a six-month million—everybody gets rich except the poor ass of a "Public Servant." (*Straight at* HASTINGS) And you've got the gall to scream because a few of your friends are smart enough to do exactly what everybody else in the country is doing.

HASTINGS How much have you been hiding from me? How much are *you* involved?

RAFFERTY About as much as you are.

HASTINGS No more clever answers, Walt. I'm calling you.

RAFFERTY Don't call me, Griff. You can't win this pot.

HASTINGS I want to know if my Attorney General is a thief. (RAFFERTY *is lighting a cigar, and we do not know at once how this accusation has affected him. Suddenly he flings*

down the burning match and approaches HASTINGS *with controlled wrath*)

RAFFERTY Don't use such graphic language with me, Mr. President! You wouldn't be in this room—you'd never have gotten your muddy shoes in the Senate cloak room—if it weren't for me!

HASTINGS I never asked for this job.

FRANCES (*Rising in her chair behind the desk*) You pleaded with him to take the nomination. The entire party wanted him.

RAFFERTY They wanted him like hell! I shoved him down the throat of that convention, like pushing a goof pill down a bucking horse's gullet, while it was biting my hand. I had to fight for every half vote. I had to buy and sell and bargain and crawl on my belly to the delegations from Nebraska and Oregon and Utah, who didn't know Griffith P. Hastings from Fatty Arbuckle!

HASTINGS "My humble servant"! You did me such a favor heading up the Justice Department where you could look out for your whole rotten gang!

RAFFERTY *Our* gang, Mr. President. The gang that makes up your margins in the stock market. The gang that knows enough about your private life to retire you from public life forever.

HASTINGS Don't threaten me! I'll demand your resignation.

RAFFERTY When the President starts accusing the Cabinet, it's the *brain* accusing the *fingers!* The head versus the right hand!

FRANCES If thy right hand offend thee, cut it off!

RAFFERTY And bleed to death? We won't let you do that to yourself, Griff!

HASTINGS I have a right to expect my appointees to conduct themselves as honorable men!

RAFFERTY When the saints come marching in, I strongly recommend that they take over the Federal Government. Until such time, the taxpayers will have to be content with human beings who are imperfect, who make mistakes, who may occasionally be swayed by "enlightened self-interest."

HASTINGS (*Crosses to desk telephone*) That's a fancy name for Grand Theft!

RAFFERTY Don't force me to do what I don't want to do, Griff. But if old friends start denouncing old friends, it could become a national pastime. It wouldn't make me happy to have you pick up a newspaper and read, not on the front page, inside somewhere, innuendos, a little hint or two—about a girl in an apartment on Gramercy Park, who entertained distinguished visitors. *A* distinguished visitor.
(HASTINGS *becomes rigid.* FRANCES *is pale; she glances from her huband to* RAFFERTY, *then back again*)

HASTINGS (*Puts down the phone*) I'll deny it.

RAFFERTY As a good newspaperman, you know that's the best way to spread a rumor. Deny it, and it goes on the front pages. They'll wheel out the eighty-four-point type they've been saving for the Second Coming! "*No* White House Love Nest!" (*An inspiration*) Tell you what you can do. Hire some third-rate novelist to write a book—to prove that the President is not the father of Claire Jones's illegitimate child!

(HASTINGS, *infuriated, leaps at* RAFFERTY *and seizes him by the throat*)

HASTINGS You son-of-a-bitch! You dirty son-of-a-bitch!
(HASTINGS *struggles with* RAFFERTY, *his hands still around his throat.* FRANCES *screams.* BELLINGHAM *comes in, white-faced*)

BELLINGHAM Mr. President—
(HASTINGS *continues to struggle with* RAFFERTY *until* BELL-INGHAM *pulls them apart. The* PRESIDENT *is trembling, his voice is husky with emotion*)

HASTINGS Well? Where's Ax? Why didn't you bring him back with you?

BELLINGHAM The police are in his room. And a squad from the Fire Department. They were too late. (*With hardly any voice at all*) Ax Maley hung himself.
(HASTINGS *is stunned with grief. He sinks to the couch in utter disbelief. Somehow there is the sense that the death of his old friend is his own death as well*)

The Curtain Falls

ACT THREE

In the darkness, we hear the PRESIDENT'S *voice over a public-address system, coming to an oratorical climax*

HASTINGS' VOICE So, my friends in this magnificent city by the Golden Gate, let us march forward together. With daring, seasoned by reasonable caution, with hearts ready to climb mountain tops, yet with feet planted solidly in the valleys of practicality, let us stand shoulder to shoulder in quest of our inevitable destiny.

(There are cheers and applause, the honking of klaxons. A band plays "Hail to the Chief." As the curtain rises, the background sky is a colorful stream of confetti, serpentine, and American flags. The effect fades away as the lights come up.)

Scene: A hotel room in San Francisco, high above Union Square. It is the following summer. This is the sumptuous sitting room of the best suite in the hotel. The decor is Louis Quinze, baroque, golden, and chandelier-ridden. A balcony upstage overlooks the square. In the center of the room is a huge brocade couch. There are several large upholstered chairs and a gilt French phone. The afternoon sun floods across the room warmly. BELLINGHAM *is on the balcony, looking down at the activity in the square below.* FRANCES *is seated in one of the downstage chairs, listening to the cheers, but staring into the distance. Her voice has a weary, wistful quality.*

FRANCES When he's up on a platform speaking to everybody, he doesn't seem much different. But when he comes back to our hotel suite, in city after city, I see how old he looks, what it's doing to him. My God, it seems like a hundred years since that hotel room in Chicago, when I begged him to take the nomination. I never imagined it would be anything like this.

BELLINGHAM (*Coming in from the balcony*) Why hasn't he said anything?

FRANCES He's running away. That's the only reason for this endless speaking tour.

BELLINGHAM What's he running away from? Is he still afraid of the stories Rafferty can start? I know how painful this is for you, Mrs. Hastings; but plenty of presidents have survived attacks on their personal lives. It wasn't so long ago half the country was singing a jingle about Grover Cleveland: "Ma, Ma, where's my Pa? Gone to the White House, ha, ha, ha." But they elected him. Twice!

FRANCES (*Closing her eyes*) Bruce, I've told him I'm not afraid of any personal scandal. He's really running away because he can't face the fact that his friends have done this.

BELLINGHAM (*Persistently*) He's got to face it. He's got to speak out. I had to beg Senator Hearn for the chance to come to San Francisco. The Senator was ready to issue subpoenas last Friday. The President can be impeached!

FRANCES Can they impeach him for trusting old friends?

BELLINGHAM Old friends are fine. For lodge meetings and class reunions. But "Government by Crony" can destroy him!

FRANCES Bruce, what can he do? (*She rises helpless, frustrated*) He blames himself so much, he can't get the words out.

BELLINGHAM Get somebody else to speak for him. Somebody he can trust.

FRANCES Arthur Anderson is here in San Francisco. I invited him. I've convinced Griffith he has to see him.

BELLINGHAM Good.

FRANCES Perhaps he'll take the Secretary into his confidence. I don't know. If he doesn't, I don't know what else to try. (*Unsteadily, she crosses to the cabinet*) Would you care for something to drink?

BELLINGHAM No thank you.

FRANCES If you don't mind.
   (FRANCES *takes a decanter of whisky from the cabinet and awkwardly pours herself a shot, spilling some. She drinks quickly, almost painfully.* BELLINGHAM *watches with quiet surprise; he's never seen her take a drink before. There are voices in the hall.* FRANCES *dabs at the spilled liquor with her handkerchief*)

HASTINGS' VOICE (*From off, heartily*) All right, fellas, the Secret Service is relieved for the day. You lucky bums can go inspect the Barbary Coast. Give me a full report.
   (*There is laughter from the hallway.* HASTINGS *comes into the room, stops short at the sight of* BELLINGHAM)

HASTINGS Bruce! (*Whereas the* PRESIDENT's *hair was silver before, now it is completely white. But this, and the other ravages of the year, seem to have given him even greater stature. He has the majesty of a man who has just been cheered by thousands of people. Some strands of serpentine and confetti still cling to his coat. He is glad to see* BELLING-HAM, *but he senses the purpose of this unexpected visit*) What are you doing in San Francisco?

BELLINGHAM (*Shaking hands with* HASTINGS) You're looking very well, Mr. President.

HASTINGS Sure, there's nothing like shaking hands with a few hundred thousand strangers to put a man in shape. (*He lifts a strand of confetti from his shoulder and dangles it*) You've got to be careful in a town where there are lots of Italians. You don't know if they're throwing confetti or spaghetti. (HASTINGS *laughs*) That's Ax's joke. (*He crosses to* FRANCES *and gives her his coat*) I know, Duchess. There never was such a person as Axel Maley. I only read about him in the funny papers. (*Suddenly, to* BELLINGHAM) Look, by God, this is lucky! Arthur Anderson's coming up in a minute. I tell you, I've got a guardian angel that sent you here to translate for me!

FRANCES You'll be able to talk more freely with Secretary Anderson if you're alone.

BELLINGHAM She's right, sir. (FRANCES *exits with the* PRESI-DENT'S *coat*)

HASTINGS Sure, sure. How about a drink? (*He crosses to the cabinet, bracing himself for what* BELLINGHAM *has to tell him.*) O.K., Bruce. What's the news?

BELLINGHAM They're trying to whitewash everything except the White House.

HASTINGS Why doesn't that damn Senator you work for stay in the Senate Office Building and answer his mail?
(*He gets highball glasses*)

BELLINGHAM   He may be the best friend you've got.

HASTINGS   Hearn? He never did me any favors. Two things this country could do without: Prohibition and Senate Investigating Committees. (*He reaches for a bottle, holding it up appraisingly*) Duchess, the maid's been nipping at the Scotch again. (*He pours two drinks, long and straight, then hands one to* BELLINGHAM) I sent Doc out to fill a prescription. But this medicinal alcohol isn't exactly Haig and Haig Pinch. (*The two men look at each other.* HASTINGS *lifts his glass in a toast*) To happier days. (*They drink*) When was the last time I saw you? At the funeral? (BELLINGHAM *nods*) The Duchess says I shouldn't have gone. How could I not go? He was my friend. Didn't Shakespeare say something like that: "Every man's death diminishes me."

BELLINGHAM   It wasn't Shakespeare, and it isn't true. Ax Maley, alive, dimished all of us.

   (HASTINGS *stares past* BELLINGHAM)

HASTINGS   I looked down into the casket and just one thing kept running through my mind: "There's them as is in and them as is out."

BELLINGHAM   You have no idea what Axel Maley did to you, Mr. President.

HASTINGS   (*Takes* BELLINGHAM'S *glass and crosses to the cabinet*) I know damn well what he did.

BELLINGHAM   And what some of your other friends have done.

HASTINGS   What does that mean?

   (BELLINGHAM *draws a photostat from his pocket.* FRANCES, *who has been listening, comes back into the room.*)

BELLINGHAM   On September fourteenth last year you signed an executive order—

HASTINGS I've signed a thousand executive orders!
(*He crosses to* BELLINGHAM *and takes the photostat, turning the pages of it quickly, searchingly*)

BELLINGHAM This one was unique. It was a very special favor for a very special friend. It allowed Secretary Loomis to give away—literally *give away*—government oil lands to private individuals for personal profit.

HASTINGS I never signed such an order! (*He pales as he reads it*) I never *understood* I was signing such an order.

BELLINGHAM I believe that, sir, but nobody else will. To Senator Hearn this is evidence that the President himself is criminally involved.

FRANCES (*Softly*) Oh, God.

BELLINGHAM There are ten thousand oil wells on government land, gushing money into private pockets, including Mr. Loomis'. It's no secret from anybody except the public. And it's not going to be a secret from them much longer. (HASTINGS *sits. The confetti-majesty vanishes like paper in a fire*) But you can still take decisive action, Mr. President. I told Hearn you're not part of any of this. He'll only believe it if you clear the record yourself. Admit that you've been sold out by your friends.

FRANCES Let Secretary Anderson say the words. You authorize him.

BELLINGHAM After Hearn lets loose his blast, anything you say will only sound defensive. Rafferty and Loomis can only stay afloat by hanging on to you. If you don't cut free, you'll sink with them.

HASTINGS I'm tired.

FRANCES Of course you're tired. You haven't eaten all day. I'll order you something.

HASTINGS No.

FRANCES What would you like? A steak, some chops?

HASTINGS No, nothing heavy. Some soup, maybe.

FRANCES Bruce?

BELLINGHAM No, thank you.
(FRANCES *goes out. Slowly* HASTINGS *raises his head, looks at* BELLINGHAM)

HASTINGS Bruce. What am I going to do? (*Without a trace of self-pity*) Back in Wilmont, once a year, they used to take the brightest kid from the junior class at the high school and make him Mayor for a Day. They'd stick a couple of phone books under him so he could reach the fountain pen. For twenty-four hours he'd run the town. But the next morning, the *real* mayor would always come back and straighten out the mess. (*With a wistful laugh*) Wouldn't it be great if tomorrow they sent me back to 11A? (*He picks up book and hands it to* BELLINGHAM) Hey, did you ever read this?

BELLINGHAM (*Looking at the title on the spine*) "A Boy's Lives of the Presidents."

HASTINGS (*Taking the book from him, leafing through it*) I've been reading about this Martin Van Buren. The way I see it, the country would have been just as well off if he'd stayed in Albany. You wouldn't call him a great President, would you?

BELLINGHAM I suppose if a President has five minutes of greatness in four years he's doing fine.

HASTINGS (*Turning to another page*) That Franklin Pierce—
he had about thirty seconds! (*He laughs; then sobers.* BEL-
LINGHAM *is silent*) I can't quit, Bruce. Who the hell can I turn
in my resignation to? God? (*The telephone rings.* HASTINGS
*crosses to the table to answer it. He puts the book on the
table*) Yes? (FRANCES *enters*) I guess so. All right, send him
up. (*Slowly he hangs up the telephone*) Arthur Anderson is
on his way up in the elevator.

BELLINGHAM I'd better go.

HASTINGS Stay! Please stay.

BELLINGHAM I'm the enemy. (*As he stares at the President,
his gaze softens*) Not really. I'm leaving the Hearn Committee.

HASTINGS (*Sitting on the arm of the couch*) Good. Get out of
politics. Smart boy.

BELLINGHAM No, sir. I'm not going to run away again. Somebody in politics has to give a damn. And I give a damn.
(*He shakes hands with the* PRESIDENT *and starts to leave*)

HASTINGS (*Stopping him*) Bruce. (BELLINGHAM *turns*) I never
really wanted to fire you.

BELLINGHAM Mr. President. I never really quit.
(*A soft smile passes between the men.* BELLINGHAM *goes
out*)

FRANCES Your soup will be up in just a few moments, dear.
(*There is a knock at the door.* FRANCES *starts to go, but
realizes her husband is tortured with uncertainty. She tries
to give him what strength she can*) Griffith, it's not as if
you had to make a decision. There's only one thing you can

do. Don't even think about me, or what they might say about us personally. It doesn't matter. (HASTINGS *just stares at her. There is another knock*) I'll leave you alone with the Secretary.

HASTINGS (*Suddenly desperate*) No, Frances. Stay here.
(*She wants to remain, as a mother wants to be with her child in a time of pain or sorrow. But she knows it will only weaken him*)

FRANCES I'd stay, I'd do anything, if I thought I could help. But I can't. I've hurt you too much already by thinking I could.
(*She goes off. The* PRESIDENT *straightens himself, and manages to put on some of the bluff, extroverted manner*)

HASTINGS (*Calling*) Come in. Come in, Mr. Secretary.
(ARTHUR ANDERSON *comes into the room. Despite the forbidding formality, he is trying to be kindly. They shake hands*)

ANDERSON How are you, Mr. President?

HASTINGS Fine, Arthur, fine. Sit down, uh—Arthur. (ANDERSON *sits*) It was very good of you to come all the way across the country like this—on such short notice.

ANDERSON From the urgency of the request, I gathered it was on a matter of major importance.

HASTINGS Well, yes, I suppose you could put it that way. (HASTINGS *sits on the couch. He picks up a newspaper, clutching it in his fists, trying to find a way to say what must be said. He squeezes the paper so hard, his knuckles are white*) How was the train trip out?

ANDERSON Warm. But endurable.

HASTINGS Glad you're here, Arthur. Glad you're here. Now. Let's get right down to the core of things. (*He reaches for the book as something to hang on to, another means for delaying what he dreads to say*) I've been reading a lot of history lately. Government. Political science. Lives of the Presidents. Mr. Secretary, I've made mistakes. But *all* of them made mistakes.

(*Even the antiseptic* ANDERSON *is touched by this. He now speaks with some awkwardness*)

ANDERSON Would you care to be more specific about anything, Mr. President?

HASTINGS (*Unable to look directly at Anderson*) Yes. Let's take one of these Presidents. What does this man do if he has based his entire political life on the reliability of friends? And if these friends—this is just imaginary, you understand —if they turn out to be unworthy of the confidence he's put in them.

(HASTINGS' *confession peters out. He's looking at the floor;* ANDERSON *is unable to watch* HASTINGS)

ANDERSON Such a man would need to call on the deepest resources of his greatness.

HASTINGS (*Exploding*) I don't understand all this talk about greatness! I didn't get elected because I was going to be some kind of one-man government. I can't do this job by myself. You've got to have faith. In the people around you. I've got faith in you, Arthur.

ANDERSON Let me help you, Mr. President. If I can.

HASTINGS All right, Arthur. Here's what I want you to do. (*He takes a deep breath*) I want you to—(*Anderson rises*)

I want you to— (*He breaks off and tries again*) I want you to—

ANDERSON   Yes, sir?

(HASTINGS' *whole body is taut. He touches his stomach, doubling over slightly, in genuine pain*)

HASTINGS   Frances! Frances!

(ANDERSON *moves to help him, but the* PRESIDENT *waves him away.* FRANCES *enters quickly.* HASTINGS *sits, his head in his hands*)

FRANCES   Yes?

HASTINGS   Frances, I seem to be—why don't you phone up Doc Kirkaby to bring over some of those white pills? I—

FRANCES   Yes, dear. (FRANCES *goes out quickly*)

HASTINGS   My stomach tightens up and I can't think. Arthur, will you be at your hotel?

ANDERSON   The St. Francis.

HASTINGS   Fine, Fine. I'll call you a little later and we'll go over these things point by point.

ANDERSON   I'll be waiting for your call. (ANDERSON *starts to leave, then stops, concerned*) I know a very good internist here; would you like me to call him?

HASTINGS   No, no. The General's right down the hall. He'll take care of it.

(FRANCES *re-enters, nodding for* ANDERSON *to leave.* ANDERSON *goes out.* HASTINGS *seems a little dazed; he hasn't fully realized that the Secretary has left. He calls after him*)

HASTINGS   Thank you, Arthur! (*He repeats numbly to himself*)   Thank you.

FRANCES Dr. Kirkaby is coming. He says that you're to lie down immediately. Undo that tight collar, Griffith.

HASTINGS It's nothing. Don't worry, I feel fine. Fine! (*Sighs*) I won't kid you, Duchess. I feel God-awful! (*He catches her hand*) I didn't tell him.
  (FRANCES *looks at him, wordlessly. There is a knock at the door*)

FRANCES Come in, Doctor.
  (DOC *enters. His uniform looks as if he had pulled it on hastily. He carries a black medical satchel, which he puts down on the coffee table*)

DOC What seems to be the trouble, Griff?
  (*He crosses to the chair, bends over the* PRESIDENT, *and takes his wrist*)

FRANCES He won't take care of himself; he hasn't had a bite to eat.

DOC (*Feeling* HASTINGS' *forehead*) You don't seem to have a fever, boy.

HASTINGS It's like somebody's made a fist inside of me and won't let go.

DOC (*Poking his own stomach*) I get the same kind of thing, Griff. When you're traveling, you've gotta expect it. It's the different water, and all that. I'll tell you what. Why don't I get some of the newspaper boys together for a few rounds of poker? That'll relax your stomach muscles.

FRANCES Is that a prescription, Doctor?

HASTINGS No poker, Doc. Thanks. Not now.

DOC (*Moving across the room*) I better call a specialist. When you don't want to play poker, you're sick. I got a medical directory in my room.

FRANCES If people will let him rest. And if he gets some food.

DOC Let's not take any chances. I'll be right back. (*He starts out, not taking his medical satchel. He stops short*) Walt!
(RAFFERTY *comes in jauntily, claps* DOC *on the shoulder as they pass in the doorway.* FRANCES *is shocked.* HASTINGS *sits up. But* RAFFERTY *is feeling his way. He studies the* PRESIDENT, *trying to gauge how much* HASTINGS *may have disclosed to* ANDERSON)

HASTINGS Who pushed the button for you?

RAFFERTY (*Pleasantly*) We're old friends, Griff. My responses are automatic.
(DOC, *sensing the tension, slips out of the room*)

DOC I'll get the medical directory.
(*He leaves*)

RAFFERTY I was a little hurt to find out you'd sent for Anderson without even consulting me. Naturally I was on the next train. Did you and Secretary Anderson have a nice chat?

HASTINGS Are you worried, Walt? Are you sweating?

RAFFERTY (*Twisting a cigarette into the holder*) No.

HASTINGS What did you come here for?

RAFFERTY I've traveled three thousand miles and you don't even ask me to sit down.

HASTINGS Tell me how you're serving the public Walt. I'm damned interested.

RAFFERTY (*Seemingly relaxed, lighting the cigarette*) We've had differences. But we've had a lot of years together. How many poker hands have we played, Griff? A thousand? Five thousand? How many fifths of bourbon have we put away? We've been good for each other, haven't we? You used to ask my advice. Sometimes you'd even take it.

HASTINGS I'm listening.

RAFFERTY There's a little mix-up with Josh, a little minor confusion over at Interior about some leases.

HASTINGS (*Picking up the photostat*) Some oil leases.

RAFFERTY Could be. Probably a bookkeeping error. But we've got a two-party system and the other boys might not look at it that way. (*Sits on couch*) However, there's a very simple solution. When the Hearn Committee starts making its big noise, we simply explain who was the author of the whole plan, who drew it up, who approved it, who recommended it for your immediate action. Just name the name.

HASTINGS Who?

RAFFERTY The Judge. Corriglione.

HASTINGS (*Rising*) I hope you've got a return ticket, Walt. (*At this point, a new power seems to be rising inside of* HASTINGS)

RAFFERTY Now, just a minute, Griff. This is the simple way. The best way. I've been giving this a lot of thought.

HASTINGS I know damn well you have.

RAFFERTY This way nobody'll get hurt.

HASTINGS Except Corriglione.

RAFFERTY What're you going to do? I like him. I've always liked him. But, Griff, don't play a gypsy fiddle for the Judge. (*In* HASTINGS' *code, the betrayal of friends is almost unthinkable. He turns on* RAFFERTY *with the power of a man who has just discovered a truth he can fight for, and a lie he can fight against. Outraged, he flings a mocking but belated indictment at his Attorney General*)

HASTINGS O.K., Walt. What'll we do next?

RAFFERTY What?

HASTINGS Something really big. Not just oil or booze or bedsheets. You want a power project to play with? Help yourself. How about grabbing off a National Park for your front yard?

RAFFERTY If you want to talk realistically, fine.
(*He rises*)

HASTINGS I'm being realistic! We're playing on the world's biggest poker table, aren't we? Let's make this a respectable pot.

RAFFERTY Don't be a damn fool, Griff.

HASTINGS (*Crossing to him*) You certainly aren't scared, are you, Walt? We've got plenty of friends left to hang. That's the normal way of doing business. Isn't that what made this country: "I'm for me and the hell with everybody else." Who'll we get rid of now? How about *you?* Are you expendable, Walt?

RAFFERTY (*Defensively*) Everything your Attorney General has done has been legal—with the blessing, approval, and signature of your Majesty, Griffith the First!

HASTINGS This sort of thing? (*He tosses the photostat aside, mocking* RAFFERTY's *tone*) Penny ante! What about your big triumph of nerve and salesmanship—manufacturing a President of the United States? Don't be modest. Take the credit, Walt. And while you're at it, take credit for the illegitimate child, too. Because you and everybody who voted for me were the parents of a bastard. A bastard idea—that anybody can be President.

(*He crosses upstage. A* WAITER *enters with a rolling table. A silver soup tureen and service is atop it*)

FRANCES I'll take it. That's all.

(FRANCES *wheels table upstage.* WAITER *leaves*)

RAFFERTY They've never sent a President to a federal penitentiary. Do you want to make history?

HASTINGS I haven't done anything dishonest.

RAFFERTY Say that. Somebody might believe you. (RAFFERTY *draws a key ring out of his pocket and begins to detach one key with studied casualness*) Suppose I invite your friend Senator Hearn to inspect my safe-deposit box. Did you ever wonder why Ax Maley's will has never been probated? I've stopped it. To protect you. (*He fingers the key*) His will is right behind this key. His entire seven-figure estate, however acquired, goes to his dear friend and benefactor, Griffith P. Hastings.

(HASTINGS *looks at* RAFFERTY, *almost as if he were seeing him for the first time. He speaks with great calm and certainty*)

HASTINGS Walt, I haven't made very many suggestions during my term in office, but I suggest that you *do* take Senator Hearn to your safe-deposit box. Show him anything you like.

RAFFERTY Do you want to be impeached? Is that what you want?

HASTINGS Walt, you're out. Out of the Administration. Out of my life.

RAFFERTY You're not that stupid. Almost, maybe. But not quite. You're not going to throw me out. Even in that sleeping little mind of yours, you can imagine what could happen.

HASTINGS Yes, I know what's going to happen. Everybody is going to see us. Exactly as we are. Both of us. And maybe we've done the country a favor, Walt. Maybe people will make sure nothing like this ever happens again. Oh, I suppose there'll always be plenty of Walt Raffertys around. But I pray to God that there'll never be another Griffith P. Hastings. (*Pause*) Good-by, Walt.

RAFFERTY Frances! Don't let him be a damned fool.

FRANCES Good-by, Walter.

RAFFERTY Before you torpedo the boat, Griff, just remember: everybody sinks together. The saints and the sons-of-bitches. And a halo is no life preserver!

(RAFFERTY *exits*)

FRANCES He won't do anything.

HASTINGS Yes, he will.

FRANCES Then don't let him! Fight him!

HASTINGS How can I? He'll wreck more than just one man. Much more.

(*She is on the verge of tears. Hurriedly, she makes an excuse to go off*)

FRANCES Lie down, dear. I'll get you a pillow.
(*She exits. Alone on the stage,* HASTINGS *closes his eyes. Then he looks up, his fists clenched, searching for support*)

HASTINGS Dear Jesus. (*As he lowers his head, he sees* DOC's *medical satchel. Without any visible emotion,* HASTINGS *crosses quickly to it, glancing over his shoulder to make certain* FRANCES *isn't coming. He looks at the labels of several bottles, and finally finds one small bottle, which seems to be what he's looking for. He puts it in his jacket pocket and crosses to the phone as* FRANCES *enters with a bed pillow. Into the phone*) This is the President. I want the newsmen sent up here. All of them. The whole press staff. All the correspondents. Everybody. Right away.
(HASTINGS *hangs up and turns to* FRANCES. *He extends his arms, palms up, helplessly. She comes to him. They embrace*)

FRANCES I did this to you.

HASTINGS Like hell. I wanted to be President, too. I never made it. I only got elected.

FRANCES I wish we were back in Wilmont.

HASTINGS Why?

FRANCES It's home.
(*There is a knock at the door*)

HASTINGS (*Letting his wife go*) Come in.
(JOHN BOYD *enters. He is alone, an open-faced young man fresh out of journalism school. He is scared stiff*)

BOYD They called the press room, sir.

HASTINGS Well, where are all the fellas?

BOYD Secretary Anderson gave them the slip, and they all went out to try to find him, and get a story out of him. They told me to just stay there and answer the phone. (*Blurting it*) I'm John Boyd, *Sacramento Bee*. It sure is an honor meeting you, Mr. President. (*Correcting his own copy, quickly*) *Surely* is an honor.

HASTINGS Well, Mr. Boyd, I've got a statement to make. You can pass this on to the old hands when they get back from finding out that Arthur Anderson doesn't have anything to tell them. (BOYD *hurriedly digs some folded copy paper and a pencil from his pocket and stands with schoolboy attentiveness*) The President has just accepted the resignation of the Attorney General—no, that's too damn polite—I have just *demanded* the resignation of the Attorney General of the United States, Mr. Walter Rafferty.

(*The boy is writing, but suddenly stops, shocked by the enormity of the story. He glances for a telephone*)

BOYD I'd better call Mr. Huckson. He's the political reporter on the *Bee*. I just answer phones. I've only been on the paper a couple of months.

(HASTINGS *crosses to him, and clasps a hand on his shoulder*)

HASTINGS Keep writing.

BOYD Yes, sir.

HASTINGS Rafferty. Two f's.

BOYD Yes, sir.

HASTINGS The President also requests Senator Hearn to make special inquiry into an executive order transferring certain government oil lands to the administration of Secretary Loomis. (*Obviously the boy is far behind.* HASTINGS *takes the paper and pencil out of his hands*) What have you got? (HASTINGS *glances at the paper, then starts writing on it himself*) Don't write "the's" and "and's." Put down the important words. Demand Hearn Investigate Loomis! (*He hands the paper and pencil back, then crosses back to the couch. This has taken an enormous toll of energy. He sinks to the couch, leaning his head back a little*) The President also directs that Charles Webster, former head of the Veterans' Bureau, be extradited to stand trial for grand theft and betrayal of the public trust. (*Closing his eyes*) Oh. The President wishes to reaffirm his complete confidence in his good friend, Judge Caesare Corriglione. (*He opens his eyes, looks over at the boy, realizing the young man's confusion. Slowly, he spells the name*) C-o-r-r-i-g-l-i-o-n-e. (BOYD *stops writing, and looks up, expecting more*) You got it?

BOYD Yes, sir.

HASTINGS Well, when I was an editor, that would have been enough for a story.
  (FRANCES *has filled the soup bowl and puts it on the table beside the big chair*)

BOYD (*Starting to move*) Thank you, sir. Thank you, Mr. President.
  (*But* BOYD *stops, turns, then wipes his hand across his suit and tentatively holds it out to the* PRESIDENT. HASTINGS *smiles and offers his hand. The boy crosses and shakes it. There is a look of real admiration in the boy's face. He almost runs out of the room.* FRANCES *crosses to* HASTINGS)

HASTINGS For the first time, I felt like a President of the United States. For about forty-five seconds. Well, that's fifteen seconds better than Franklin Pierce.
  (FRANCES *takes his hand, touches his face*)

FRANCES I'm proud of you. I'm very proud of you.

HASTINGS (*Staring after the departed* BOYD) Frances, I can't let school kids read in a history book that the President of the United States was a criminal. (*His hand touches the outside of his jacket pocket*) Frances, do me a favor. Get me my robe, will you?

FRANCES Of course. (FRANCES *moves quickly toward the other room. He watches her. The instant she's out of sight, he rises, reaches into his pocket, takes out the bottle, uncaps it, and dumps the contents into the soup. He thrusts the empty bottle back into his pocket. Slowly he stirs the soup, staring at it. Then he takes a spoonful, then another, increasing the tempo.* FRANCES *re-enters, carrying a gold brocade dressing gown. She helps him off with his jacket and into the dressing gown. He continues to sip the soup*) Griffith, that should be piping.

HASTINGS No. This is fine. Frances. Sit down here.

FRANCES (*Takes his coat and puts it on the couch*) I'm going to call down and ask them—

HASTINGS (*Urgently*) Frances, sit down.

FRANCES There's some toast on the cart. I could break it into croutons.

HASTINGS Frances!
  (DOC *enters, with an open medical directory in his hands*)

DOC Say, I got the number of this specialist. A Dr. Leinfelder. They say he's the best.
  (HASTINGS *tips up the soup bowl and finishes it entirely.* DOC *and* FRANCES *watch him.* HASTINGS *hands the empty soup bowl to* FRANCES)

HASTINGS (*With a faint smile*) Don't take him away from the sick people. (*He sinks into the chair*) I feel fine now, General.
(*The full light of the sunset is on his face*)

DOC You sure, boy?

HASTINGS I haven't felt this good in a long time. Had to have some food, that's all. Can't run the Lizzie without some gas in the tank.

DOC Yeah. Well, if you need me—

HASTINGS Frances'll call.

DOC (*Crossing to get his satchel*) Griff. Get some rest if you can.

HASTINGS I'll try.

DOC So long, boy.
(DOC *goes out. Now the pretense falls away and* HASTINGS *sags a little, closing his eyes*)

FRANCES (*Worried*) What's the matter, dear?

HASTINGS (*With an effort, he opens his eyes, speaking against the pressure of time*) Frances, I haven't been feeling great, off and on. Arthur Anderson knows. Doc'll swear to it. So if anything happens to me, it won't be too much of a surprise.
(*She sits on the footstool next to him*)

FRANCES You haven't been taking proper care of yourself.

HASTINGS (*Insistently*) Afterward, don't let them do an autopsy. Make sure.

FRANCES Don't say that. Don't even think that.

HASTINGS (*Suddenly alarmed*) What did you do with my jacket? (*She rises and crosses toward it*) Take the bottle out of the pocket. Get rid of it. (*Confused,* FRANCES *follows his directions. But when she sees the empty bottle, she freezes*) Don't let Doc know where I got it. He'd feel bad.

FRANCES (*As the realization strikes her*) God. Oh, God!
(FRANCES *starts to rush toward the outside door to call after* DOC, *but* HASTINGS *stops her, commandingly*)

HASTINGS Frances! (*She stops. He reaches out his hand, weakly. The dying light of the sun is on his face*) Don't spoil my chance to be on a two-cent stamp!
(*She hesitates, then slowly turns and crosses back. She sinks to her knees and embraces him. He closes his eyes and there is a moment of peace: perhaps he has been able to save the dignity of the high office he never wanted*)

The Curtain Falls

ABOUT THE AUTHORS

JEROME LAWRENCE and ROBERT E. LEE have had worldwide acclaim as playwrights. Both were born in Ohio, Lawrence in Cleveland, Lee in Elyria. Lawrence was a Phi Beta Kappa and the campus prize playwright at Ohio State University; Lee was something of a boy-genius astronomer at Ohio Wesleyan.

Lawrence was working as a writer at CBS, both in Hollywood and New York, Lee was a director at Young and Rubicam, when they met. Together they wrote some of radio's most notable dramas, two of which won Peabody Awards. Lee wrote the first book on television, Lawrence's text on radio writing was used in many universities throughout the country. They were two of the founding fathers of the Armed Forces Radio Services, and originated many of the celebrated round-the-world programs; they wrote and directed the official Army-Navy programs for D-Day, V-E Day, and V-J Day. They have written many songs, record albums, and one-act operas. Their short stories have appeared in *The Saturday Evening Post* and their short plays in many anthologies.

Their first Broadway play was *Look, Ma, I'm Dancin'!* which ran for seven months. *Inherit the Wind,* the third-longest-running serious play in the history of the American theater, has won many prizes and has been presented throughout the world, having been translated into twenty-six languages. Their other plays include the fabulously successful *Auntie Mame, The Laughmaker,* and *Only in America.*